# JOURNAL FOR THE STUDY OF THE OLD TESTAMENT
## SUPPLEMENT SERIES
# 148

JSOT Press
Sheffield

# IN SEARCH OF 'ANCIENT ISRAEL'

## Philip R. Davies

Journal for the Study of the Old Testament
Supplement Series 148

Copyright © 1992 Sheffield Academic Press

Published by JSOT Press
JSOT Press is an imprint of
Sheffield Academic Press Ltd
The University of Sheffield
343 Fulwood Road
Sheffield S10 3BP
England

Typeset by Sheffield Academic Press
and
Printed on acid-free paper in Great Britain
by Billing & Sons Ltd
Worcester

British Library Cataloguing in Publication Data

A catalogue record for this book is available
from the British Library

ISSN 0309-0787
ISBN 1-85075-380-6

# CONTENTS

## ACKNOWLEDGMENTS

I have written this book for students rather more than for my colleagues, for scholars of the future rather than for those of the past or present. Hence a certain amount of repetition, since students have more time to read. I have also tried to make each chapter as self-contained as is possible, so that it can be be set as a class assignment or as an alternative to a nightly sleeping draught. There is also a conscious frugality in the citation of secondary scholarship. One very good reason for this is that there exists a fully annotated and extensively argued treatment of the archaeological data relevant to my thesis, namely T.L. Thompson's *The Early History of the Israelite People* (Leiden, 1992), which any reader allured by my rather sketchy ideas ought to consult for the documentation of many things that I either take for granted or assert with modest appeal to the evidence. It is thanks to this large book that mine can be so short!

But I am also richly indebted to many others too. Partly because of the lack of adequate formal acknowledgement in the text to an enormous debt to the research of others, I ought to mention the names of some scholars with whom either I have discussed the subject-matter of this book or by whose ideas and writings I have been strongly influenced. For the argument of this book is neither original nor the product of one fevered brain. Among that small percentage to whom I can remember being indebted, I should mention Gösta Ahlström, Graeme Auld, Joseph Blenkinsopp, Ehud Ben Zvi, Athalya Brenner, Robert Carroll, David Clines, Robert Coote, Diana Edelman, Israel Finkelstein, Giovanni Garbini, David Gunn, Axel Knauf, Bernhard Lang, Niels-Peter Lemche, Wayne McCready, Jacob Neusner, Lori Rowlett, Thomas Thompson, John Van Seters, and Keith Whitelam. Acknowledgement is also due to my colleagues on the IOUDAIOS network, who more than compensate for the disappearance of the Senior Common Room from most of British academic life and whose erudition, imagination and humour (sometimes) have turned my computer into a conversation partner. Space forbids a full list of credits; several others might be added, and they are invited to apply for a personal oral apology. I have tried in this book to do justice to what I think their research (and I hope that of many others) implies. I apologize for not having done better justice to the work that these and many other scholars are doing, and I can only encourage them to continue making clearer by their continued research what it is I am trying to do and wanted to say. Finally, as the saying goes, for errors and defects I am alone responsible, though but for the time and scholarship donated with typical generosity by John Rogerson in reading through the final draft and supplying me with some invaluable criticism and bibliography, there would have been many more.

# ABBREVIATIONS

| | |
|---|---|
| AB | Anchor Bible |
| *AJSL* | *American Journal of Semitic Languages and Literatures* |
| *ANET* | *Ancient Near Eastern Texts Relating to the Old Testament* (3rd edition) |
| *BAR* | *Biblical Archaeology Review* |
| CHJ | The Cambridge History of Judaism |
| CRINT | Compendium Rerum Iudaicarum ad Novum Testamentum |
| DJD(J) | Discoveries in the Judaean Desert (of Jordan) |
| HDR | Harvard Dissertations in Religion |
| HSS | Harvard Semitic Studies |
| *HTR* | *Harvard Theological Review* |
| *HUCA* | *Hebrew Union College Annual* |
| ICC | International Critical Commentary |
| *IEJ* | *Israel Exploration Journal* |
| *JBL* | *Journal of Biblical Literature* |
| *JJS* | *Journal of Jewish Studies* |
| *JNES* | *Journal of Near Eastern Studies* |
| *JSOT* | *Journal for the Study of the Old Testament* |
| JSOTS | *Journal for the Study of the Old Testament*, Supplement Series |
| *KTU* | *Die Keilalphabetischen Texte aus Ugarit* |
| *NTS* | *New Testament Studies* |
| *RB* | *Revue biblique* |
| SAOC | Studies in Ancient Oriental Civilization |
| *SJOT* | *Scandinavian Journal of the Old Testament* |
| SBLMS | Society of Biblical Literature Monograph Series |
| SBT | Studies in Biblical Theology |
| SVT | Supplements to *Vetus Testamentum* |
| SWBA | The Social World of Biblical Antiquity |
| *VT* | *Vetus Testamentum* |
| WBC | Word Biblical Commentary |
| *ZAH* | *Zeitschrift für Althebraistik* |
| *ZAW* | *Zeitschrift für die alttestamentliche Wissenschaft* |
| *ZDPV* | *Zeitschrift des Deutschen Palästina-Vereins* |

Chapter One

PRELIMINARIES

*Shifting paradigms*

'In Search of Ancient Israel' may strike some readers as an innocent
title, such as might dignify a lavishly illustrated account of
archaeological discoveries revealing the life and times of biblical folk.
To others, possessors maybe of a dozen or so 'Histories of Israel' it
may seem perverse or pompous: why presume to 'search' for what
others have found, and indeed described *ad nauseam*? The truth (if an
author has any proprietorial interest in this matter) lies elsewhere.
For me, the search is not for a mislaid object, as in a treasure hunt,
but for something altogether more puzzling. And like many such
searches, it does not necessarily find what it thought it was looking
for, but something else.

This is a book about history, though it is not another 'History of
Israel': that genre is probably obsolete. Previous scholarship has left
us with an 'ancient Israel', which I shall designate with quotation
marks in order to distinguish it from the biblical Israel and the
historical Israel. For I shall be dealing with three Israels: one is
literary (the biblical), one is historical (the inhabitants of the northern
Palestinian highlands during part of the Iron Age) and the third,
'ancient Israel', is what scholars have constructed out of an
amalgamation of the two others.

Historical research into the biblical literature and into Israel at the
end of the twentieth century now has to take account of movements in
the discipline of biblical criticism over the last few decades. To my
mind, the most important of these are literary and sociological (or
anthropological)[1]. The impact of literary criticism on biblical studies

---

1    I am unable to find an agreed or satisfactory distinction. Where, for example,
sociology is understood as 'the anthropology of industrialized societies', and in view
of the existence of social anthropology, it is hard to see that there is any substantive

has acquainted most of us with the distinction between real and implied authors and real and implied readers, and with the need for a proper and precise terminology in analysing literary narratives: plot, characterization, point of view, stock scenes, types, and so on. Awareness of the text first and foremost as a literary artifact has replaced the instinct to know its author, time, place and purpose. Where this sophistication has percolated into University and college curricula, it is now much easier for a student to appreciate that the deity who destroys Sodom and Gomorrah and the fish that swallows Jonah are each characters in a narrative constructed by an author, and, as the phrase goes, any resemblance to real or actual persons or events may be purely coincidental. There is no way in which history automatically reveals itself in a biblical text; there are no *literary* criteria for believing David to be more historical than Joshua, Joshua more historical than Abraham, and Abraham more historical than Adam. An additional problem, in fact, is that there is no *non-literary* way of making this judgment either, since none of these characters has left a trace outside the biblical text! Even within the text, the David of 1 Samuel is not the David of 2 Samuel, literarily speaking. These are two characters, created by (probably) different authors. How can it be possible for an historian to conflate them or choose between them with any degree of assurance or justification?

We have become at least able, if not all of us willing, to accept the premise that any character or event in the Bible is in the first instance (and possibly the last) a *literary* character or event. This does not mean, of course, that they are unrelated to history in some way–and the ways are numerous! But it does mean, or it ought to mean, that we are inclined to be more cautious about confusing literature and history. Nothing in a literary text is necessarily or automatically real outside the text, unless we include the author's head. Now, the search for 'ancient Israel' starts off precisely with that simple but unavoidable distinction in mind: the object of the search is quite boldly and extensively drawn in the Bible, and no search is needed to find Israel's ancestors, its history, its religion, its deity and its hopes. These lie on the page, and to read them is to find them. They require no filling out, no rationalising, no defence. As a literary construct, Israel is no more and no less than what the writers have made it, and

demarcation. Indeed, even 'sociology' tends to be defined differently in British and North American cultures.

if the picture is contradictory or confusing, that is not to be objected to in a literary work. Many biblical scholars who practise literary criticism are quite content to leave the matter there; indeed, some of them display a certain amount of anti-historical feeling–or at the very least agnosticism or pessimism or apathy regarding the historical Israel. I can quite sympathize with this approach: historical research need have no bearing on the way a critic chooses to read a text. But if the reader decides to assume the identity of an historian, then reader-response, the meaning of the text, and history come together. It's a matter of choice, and it is a choice I have taken here.

But the discipline of history itself has been affected by work done in literary criticism. Historians[2] today (as in classical times) are aware of the elusiveness of 'history' in an objective sense. History is a narrative, in which happenings and people are turned into events and characters. This is true of our own memories, which select experiences and order them into a narrative sequence, selecting, interpreting and distorting. The result has a narrative form, and includes not just external events but internal feelings, impressions and value-judgments. Whenever we try to understand the past we indulge in story-telling. No story, and that includes the stories our memories generate, is ever an innocent representation of the outside world. All story is fiction, and that must include historiography. The historian may like to invest trust in these stories, but should never avoid the question 'why is this story being told?' The answer can never be 'because what it describes happened', for not only is that untrue, since stories do not neatly reproduce 'what happened', but the fact of something happening does not of itself provide an adequate reason for telling it. Literature is a form of persuasive communication, and it cannot help conveying its author. Most literary critics would accept that in a broad (for some even a narrow) sense literature is ideology. If so, historiography, as a branch of literature, is also ideology. Certainly, no-one can pretend that today our own understanding of the past is highly influenced by the stories of others that we hear or read. Our understanding of the past cannot be independent of others'. A modern historian confronting the biblical text must ask what it is (s)he is being asked to believe, and ask her- or himself why it should be believed. It is not enough for an historian to trust the text or its

2    Philosophers also, of course: see e.g. A. Danto, *Analytical Philosophy of History*, Cambrige: CUP, 1965.

unknown author. The historian has to be trusted too, and credulity does not become an historian. If all historians are inescapably bound to tell a story and not 'the facts', then at least this story must be our own.

The practice of history-writing among biblical scholars has also been influenced by methods used in the social sciences, including the application of models, theories of social formation and change, and the use of the concepts of ideal types and roles to analyze behaviour. Some scholars have protested that such methods are not appropriate. In particular, they argue that sociology or anthropology is not a science which formulates laws, that social behaviour is not predictable. Some also argue that models applied in biblical studies are unverifiable, while comparative studies are invalid. There is no opportunity here to discuss these criticisms. Instead, I might point out some common ground. First, it *is* meaningful to talk about societies and not merely collections of individuals. Durkheim's 'social facts' are real enough, and are regularly vindicated in our society's use of statistics to predict human behaviour. One cannot predict an individual's behaviour, but can predict that of a group, as the social sciences regularly show. This poses a philosophical paradox, but it is true that people as groups behave differently from people as individuals: here is a kind of social-scientific quantum theory. Second: individuals acquire their identity from their position within society; they learn values from their parents and peers and internalize their own status and class, behaving accordingly. Third, knowledge is a social possession, and can be used to bestow or withhold power. Any reflective person living in Great Britain is aware of the paranoia that its governments display over the kind of access to information that citizens of the United States enjoy.

I can summarize the net effect of the preceding observations thus: authors have individual, group and class interests. Every text will reflect something of its own social context, and that reflection will always be subjective. No piece of literature, any more than any individual human perception, is an objective portrayal of what we call the 'real world'. The surface of the mirror is always distorted, and we cannot conceptualize the image which is being reflected unless we examine the surface of the mirror. 'Hermeneutic of suspicion' is an infelicitous phrase, since suspicion tends to be a pejorative term. Yet all writing deceives, of necessity, in the sense that it tends to represent as real something that is not. Texts cannot reproduce reality except as a textual artifact, crafted by rhetoric and limited by the boundaries of language. That must be true of the biblical text too. Where a comparison of literary portraits is possible, the different subjectivities can be amalgamted into a hyper-subjective (but not objective) portrait. But not where, as with the biblical literature, there is but one image.

The literary and sociological innovations in biblical studies have had a deeper effect than is often recognized. This effect might be called a humanizing one. Both approaches have challenged the sense of transcendental reality which has always lain just below the surface of most biblical research, as if the scholar were dealing at first or second hand with ultimate reality (called God) or some kind of definitive revelation from him/her/it. Both literary criticism and sociology are human-centred and to some extent relativistic; at least they are non-metaphysical. Recognizing that the biblical literature is, like any literature, a distorting product of human authors (and it would be distorting even if it were written by a deity, since deities have to use our language and have to have a point of view) lays the ground for what I hesitate to call a 'paradigm shift'. But something of the sort is indeed occurring. We are enjoying a climate in which a non-theological paradigm is beginning to claim a place alongside the long-dominant theological one (which will never be replaced).[3] The new

3    The influence of theology on biblical studies has been addressed several times in recent writing, for example in N. Gottwald's *The Tribes of Yahweh. A Sociology of the Religion of Liberated Israel 1250-1050 BCE*, Maryknoll: Orbis, 1979, pp. 667-709, which nevertheless continues the programme of the 'Biblical Theology' movement and in my view (and that of most reviewers) uses history as a mode of theology. While I admire some aspects of Gottwald's work, it is hard to see how his own agenda can be pursued by those who arrive at different historical reconstructions. G. Garbini, *History and Ideology in Ancient Israel*, London: SCM Press, 1988, also attacks (particularly German) theologians, but gives no systematic account of the foundations of his own approach to the biblical literature, which seems to combine a rigorous scepticism with the oddest flights of fancy. The most lucid discussion of the problem is by R. Oden, *The Bible Without Theology*, San Francisco: Harper and Row, 1987; pp. 1-39 contain a sound critique of the 'tradition' of biblical historical-critical studies and pp. 154-62 appeal for an alternative method of biblical study to be exploited alongside the theological one. A review of the effects of biblical and theological vocabulary on the discipline of biblical studies itself can also be found in my 'Does Biblical Studies Need a Dictionary?' in D.J.A. Clines *et al.* (ed.),*The Bible in Three Dimensions*, Sheffield: JSOT Press, 1990, pp. 321-35.

paradigm emerges by the simple effort of demonstrating that the old paradigm *is* a paradigm, sustained by consent and claiming truth for itself. Being non-theological, it can renounce any interest in the historicity or non-historicity of what the literature says, and also in the literary or ethical value of what is said. It must, however, persuade by offering an alternative way of understanding the literature which is sufficiently inclusive to function as a working hypothesis. In this book I have tried to do this, though only by bringing together the work of many other scholars. According the new paradigm, there is a need for a genuine search for 'ancient Israel', which under the old paradigm had been taken for granted– indeed, it was a necessary assumption and therefore not open to question.

### 'Ancient Israel'

As mentioned earlier, I am construing 'ancient Israel' as a scholarly construct. It is not the Israel of the biblical literature, as I shall argue. The 'ancient Israel' about which biblical scholars write draws very deeply on the biblical Israel and has its own history and a religion, which, according to its proponents has left relics of its past in Palestine. But unlike the biblical Israel, which the reader brings to life by reading the biblical text, the scholarly 'ancient Israel' lies between literature and history–or rather, it straddles the two. It is elusive and hence it needs to be sought. The search for 'ancient Israel' is all the more important since it is often spotted, but rarely pinned down. Hence, for example, archaeologists digging west of the Jordan river are frequently claiming, or denying, that they have uncovered traces of 'ancient Israel', that such and such a sherd or homestead or seal is, or is not, 'Israelite'. But to me, at any rate, such a claim, or such a denial, makes no sense unless there are archaeological criteria for making the distinction. And what might such criteria be? Archaeologically, we cannot establish what the distinctive cultural characteristics of 'ancient Israel' are. Indeed, it is a moot point whether, in the absence of the biblical literature, archaeology would have discovered any 'ancient Israel' at all. It has, of course, discovered new population centres in the early Iron Age, but it has no *archaeological* reason to call these 'Israel'. Archaeologists and historians have evidence of a state called 'Judah' but have no *archaeological* reason to regard this state as having anything to do with 'Israel' unless they happen to believe that this state was incorporated into the state of Israel which adjoined it to the north. This 'northern kingdom', as we are accustomed to refer to it, is the only 'Israel' which an archaeologist or historian, as opposed to biblical interpreter, can encounter, and it existed in the northern and central Palestinian highlands between roughly the ninth and precisely the late eighth centuries BCE. This is the Israel, in other words, which has left its traces in the soil of Palestine over a couple of centuries. This is the *historical* Israel (and so it does not need quotation marks). And, like the biblical Israel, it is not the same as the 'ancient Israel' of which our learned textbooks and monographs tell us.

This 'ancient Israel, I repeat, is both literary, in that it takes its point of departure from the biblical Israel, and historical, in that scholars treat of its interaction with other states, its political evolution, and so on. But it is a mixture of two different sorts of entity, and as such is something *sui generis*; neither biblical nor historical. It is the result, to be precise, of taking a literary construct and making it the object of historical investigation. In seeking to impose (I use the word carefully) what is *literary* upon a time and place that are *historical*, biblical scholarship and its own 'ancient Israel' betray both literature and history, and vindicate the charge that 'biblical history' is indeed neither biblical nor history.

In this book, I am searching in the first instance for what scholars *think* exists. But if, instead of assuming beforehand that a literary construct necessarily has an historical existence, we keep an open mind and try to establish whether or not that is the case, we shall find that it is very hard to define or describe. We can write a history of biblical Israel, although no paraphrase can enhance the biblical text itself; and we can write a (sketchy) history of the historical Israel, which occupied the central Palestinian highlands for just over two centuries. Neither of these two Israels presents any problem of conception. The scholarly 'ancient Israel', on the other hand, does. And the situation is more complicated still, since this scholarly projection, this literary-historical hybrid, is also posited as the producer of the biblical literature–in other words as the creator of the biblical Israel. But if, as I am going to argue, there *is* no such 'ancient Israel' which 'wrote the Bible', then we have to ask who *did* 'write the Bible' and thus produce its (literary) Israel? To the conventional biblical scholar that is a rhetorical question which merely confirms the need for the hypothesis of an 'ancient Israel'. Yet I ask it as a real and serious question. The search for 'ancient Israel' is a genuine and important one, and it leads in the end to the fundamental question: where did the biblical literature come from, and why and when was it produced? What shall stand in the gap left by the demise of 'ancient Israel'? Who produced one of the most influential ideas ever to emerge in history–the biblical Israel, an idea that has been making history for two thousand years? The search in this book ends with only the beginning of an answer to that basic question.

## Summary of the argument

The next chapter deals with 'ancient Israel' and with its creators. It is thus not solely about an hypothesized entity but also about a discipline and its practitioners. Then I shall deal (chapter three) with the Israel(s) of the biblical literature, and emphasize that it is (they are) from the point of view of an historian quite incoherent and self-contradictory, which is no criticism at all so long as the interpreter is not trying to make them historical. Next (chapter four), I shall examine the third, historical Israel, the people who lived in a kingdom that bore the name, in Iron Age Palestine but whose resemblance to the biblical Israel is superficial and not substantive. In chapter five I shall try and ascribe the biblical 'Israel', in a rather approximate manner, to an historical society at a particular time, looking for the historical context of the writing. At this juncture what is emerging is an alternative to 'ancient Israel' in the form of the historical society that really generated the literary Israel.

From this point onwards, we are no longer looking for any kind of Israel, but for a society which, in producing the literary Israel, is seeking to create for itself an identity it does not yet have (chapter seven). For what purposes and under what conditions did this society create this Israel, obviously as a projection of itself?

The authorship of the biblical literature has often been presented in biblical scholarship as a corporate entity: it is said to enshrine the 'faith of Israel', nourished and developed by 'the community', its ultimate form lovingly and tellingly shaped by a 'canonical process'. However eloquent or theologically useful this view may be, it emerges in the light of historical or sociological reflection, or even plain common sense, as fantastical.[4] The authors who, in my view, replace this 'ancient Israel' are not a society, nor are they a 'community' of the same kind. Quite apart from the absence of an Iron Age society resembling 'ancient Israel', and which could therefore have created the biblical Israel, it is obvious that literature in the ancient world is not the product of a whole society; it is a scribal activity and thus confined to less than five per cent of any ancient agrarian society. Of the remaining ninety-five per cent, most of those who had any literacy could not acquire or study this kind of literature, and it is hard to imagine that the peasants, had they the gift of literacy, would have had either the leisure or enthusiasm to exploit something that hardly addressed their own priorities. So whatever the name given to the authors of the biblical literature, they are a small and élite class, and their creation, 'Israel', a reflection of their class consciousness (to use a Marxian term). Whatever actual religion (if any) the biblical literature reflects, it is not the religion of people outside this class; and it remains to be demonstrated that the members of the class itself *had* a religion which the biblical literature could be taken to represent.

The next question (chapter eight) is to ask in what sense, if at all, the biblical literature may helpfully be categorized as 'religious' rather than reflecting a typical eastern Mediterranean culture in which secularity is a meaningless concept. Given the world-view of societies in which social life, health, weather, and historical disaster involved

---

4    It may be conceded that Brevard Childs, the most famous 'canon(ical) critic' was not essential concerned with intentionality, even at the canonical level. However, this is certainly not how several of his students have developed his work, and he himself has been at times ambiguous on this. See B.S. Childs, *Introduction to the Old Testament as Scripture*, London: SCM Press, 1979. For a recent discussion and evaluation, see M.G. Brett, *Biblical Criticism in Crisis*, Cambridge: CUP, 1991. To my mind, the real danger of this kind of approach is not that it is unhistorical but that in the hands of scholars other than Childs, it becomes a means of privileging a confessional-theological interpretation, on the grounds that literature produced by 'communities of faith' is legitimately addressed to them–and, implicitly, that those outside such communities are guilty of reading 'against' the 'message' of the text. I prefer to see a theological reading as a legitimate option among others, and based not on a claim about the objective character of its contents but on the decision of the Church (or synagogue, though this is really a Christian problem) to adopt this literature as a canon. I can see, of course, that to many Protestants this is an impossible concession but religious commitments should not parade as scholarly methods.

the gods, and thus in which 'non-religious' was a virtually empty category, it is not necesary to assume that the biblical literature was originally written in the service of a particular cult or for the purposes of devotional study or liturgical recitation, and certainly not necessarily regulative or authoritative for the belief and conduct of a religious community or tradition. Exploring why and how the biblical literature was composed and how it functioned entails first of all recognizing the possibility of a distinction between the creation of the literature itself and the adoption of it as the scripture of a religious system. It is indeed possible that the literature was composed as religious scripture in the first place, but such an assumption requires the prior existence of such a religious system. The Bible, of course, was self-evidently not written as a canon of scripture: a canon is a product of selection; of adoption, not of writing. No author of any biblical literature can be described as a 'biblical author' except by means of a kind of shorthand. No author of this literature was writing 'scripture'. Now if we cannot establish that in the period before Christianity and rabbinic Judaism were formed there was no single 'Judaism' based on 'scripture', it becomes very unlikely that the biblical writings ever were the expression of a normative religion, if any religion at all. The process by which 'literature' becomes what we call 'scripture' is a crucial and hitherto largely ignored one which needs to be raised, even if it cannot as yet be answered competently.

In my own view, the biblical literature almost certainly must have emerged as a political-cultural product of the Jerusalem 'establishment' (a loose term which I will try and define more closely at the proper time), based in the temple there, though perhaps also in the court of the governor. By a series of processes, several of which can be plausibly reconstructed, this literature became definitive of a traditional culture among certain classes, and in particular came to be adopted by groups wishing to adopt a 'Judaean' lifestyle. Although inevitably such literature will have been concerned with the role of a deity or deities, cult practice, cosmogony, prophetic records and wisdom sayings, that does not immediately place it in the category of 'scripture'. But in many cases, the lifestyle sought was a religious one, or became more and more religiously defined, and the literature that was to become the Bible began to assume among such groups the functions of what we call 'scripture'.

The final chapter of this book suggests a further step in the establishment of the biblical literature as the 'writings of the Jews', in which the biblical literature achieved a fixed and authoritative status (though how far this status was essentially religious is not certain). But a political decision to institute this literature as a national archive explains the fixation of a standard text and establishes a set number of books that can subsequently be 'canonized'.

Chapter Two

## SEARCHING FOR 'ANCIENT ISRAEL'

I defined 'ancient Israel' in the previous chapter as the product of scholars, and the focus of this chapter is biblical scholarship. I want to ask here why it has been taken for granted that 'ancient Israel' is an accessible historical entity, and to examine some of the hermeneutical practices of biblical historians which arise from, and subsequently protect, this assumption. I am suggesting that there is no searching for the *real* (historical) ancient Israel because such a search is not thought to be necessary; but the thesis of this book is that a search *is* necessary, since 'ancient Israel' is *not* an historical construct, and that it therefore has displaced something that *is* historical. Then I shall look at a few logical problems inherent in the practice of biblical historical scholarship, and finally suggest whether what I have diagnosed about the discipline is explicable by the particular interests of its practitioners.

### What are we looking for?

The search for an historical 'ancient Israel' has formed no part of the agenda of biblical scholarship for a long while. The object has never been missing; indeed, it has never been defined. It has been taken for granted that 'ancient Israel' is *there*, historically speaking, and that scholarship's business is finding out its when, why and wherefore, dotting its 'i's and crossing its 't's. Occasionally, it is true, scholars explicate this or that *biblical* concept of Israel, be it the Deuteronomist's or the Chronicler's, and imply that there is an amount of idealization in them, but rarely if ever is it asked whether there really ever existed a social and political reality which these concepts reflect, elaborate and 'idealize'. I do not believe it would occur to most scholars that the existence of an historical 'ancient Israel' needed to be questioned. Yet, after all, what biblical scholarship takes for granted, and calls 'ancient Israel', is really prescribed and defined only in the biblical literature itself. Indeed, as I shall try to demonstrate, there is no other source from which such an entity could be defined.[1] This source, however, the biblical literature, quite definitely and precisely offers us a *literary construct*, though one that is given a (sometimes vague) geographical and temporal setting in an historical world, presented as a society historically, religiously and ethnically continuous and living in Palestine[2] from at least the beginning of what we now term the Iron Age (c. 1250–600 BCE; biblical scholars more commonly use the term 'pre-exilic' or 'monarchic' when speaking of this era).

Now, despite its exclusively biblical starting point, the scholarly 'ancient Israel' differs from the biblical Israel quite a lot. The story of the biblical Israel goes all the way back to the creation of the world, where its institutions are already foreshadowed: Elohim celebrates a sabbath when he makes the world; animals are divided into clean and unclean; humans call upon the god Yahweh, who is the creator of the world. The nation itself starts life with Abraham, or, more precisely, with Jacob, and its story ends (somewhere in the fifth century BCE) with the activity of Ezra and/or Nehemiah. Non-biblical writings, of course, and the New Testament, take the story of 'Israel' further, but

---

1    I use both 'biblical literature' and 'Bible' to refer to the contents of the Tenakh/Hebrew Bible/Old Testament (excluding the literature in the apocrypha and the New Testament), mainly in order to avoid the questions of definition encountered in 'Old Testament' and 'Hebrew Bible'. I distinguish between 'biblical literature' and 'Bible' as follows: the former denotes the literature, where conceived as a whole or in part, while the latter denotes this literature conceived or instituted as a body of religious scriptures or a canon. I use the adjective 'biblical' (lower case) when referring merely to the literature and 'Biblical' (upper case) when I mean the literature as a religious corpus.

2    'Palestine' is the term used for this territory since at least Assyrian times (cf. *ANET*, p. 281), but some scholars find it unacceptable, mainly for reasons connected with contemporary Middle Eastern politics, but also because linguistically it is thought to imply Philistines. But it has never really carried that implication. The increasingly common alternative, 'land of Israel', is unsuitable because only a small part of Palestine was ever occupied, and for a short time, by a state called 'Israel'. I have considered the neutral term 'Cisjordan', as used by e.g. D. Edelman ('Introduction,' *SJOT* 2 [1991], pp. 3-6), but the term is unfamiliar to many readers; perhaps in time it will become the accepted nomenclature. I certainly disclaim interest in any political argument in this book.

in this book I am confining myself to the Hebrew Bible, or Old Testament.

Now, scholarship has never regarded this biblical 'Israel'[3] as a literary construct, but has treated it as an historical one. This historical version of the literary 'Israel' is what I am referring to (with most scholars) as 'ancient Israel'. The timespan of the biblical story, roughly from Abraham to Ezra, is called the 'biblical period'.[4] Such terms betray the extent to which the literary has been assimilated to the historical in biblical criticism, and it is worthwhile pondering this phenomenon for a moment. After all, the naming of a period after the literature in which it is described is, from the historian's point of view, a bit misleading, however natural is seems to the biblical scholar. The literature itself was at least largely compiled into its present form, and at most almost entirely written, at a time later than this 'biblical period', during the rule of the Persians and then the Hellenistic monarchies. It would surely be strictly accurate to call *this* epoch the 'biblical period'.[5] But biblical scholars do no such thing: the 'biblical period' remains in our learned (as well as popular) conversation the time *before* the biblical literature *as we have it* was written. It denotes, in other words, the period to which that literature *refers*. Now, when we express that period in dates, say from the Late Bronze age to the fifth century BCE, we are delineating a quantifiable historical period. However, if we express the epoch as 'from Abraham to Ezra' we are doing something quite different: for not only are we unable to assign precise dates to these characters, but also we are making the assumption that literary figures and events placed in an historical context (however vague) rightly belong there, indeed,

---

3    It is of course true that there is no single biblical 'Israel'; there are (sometimes important) differences between its books. However, there is enough basic agreement between them to justify, at least for the moment, the singular number. My argument is not affected by the recognition that the biblical literature is not unanimous in all points.

4    A. Mazar's *Archaeology of the Land of the Bible* (AB), Garden City: Doubleday, 1990, comprises a history from the Neolithic period until 586 BCE, most of this period irrelevant to the Bible, and in any case stopping short before any biblical literature as we have it was composed. A somewhat parallel usage to 'biblical period' occurs in the modern Hebrew/Israeli designations for the Bronze and Iron Age, respectively 'Canaanite period' and 'Israelite period'.

5    Thus already Morton Smith, *Palestinian Parties and Politics That Shaped the Old Testament*, second edition London: SCM Press, 1987, p. 7.

constitute the period itself. And, whatever may be our decision regarding the historicity of Abraham or of Ezra, biblical scholars have set this literary Israel into the historical period to which the biblical literature rather vaguely assigns it, and have then written about it pretty directly as an historical entity. The 'biblical period' thus assumes an historical objectivity, regardless of the reliability or accuracy of the literature to which the period properly belongs. It would not be unfair to say that until recently, 'Histories of Israel' virtually rewrote the biblical story with a mildly rationalistic tone. Into this 'biblical period', and indeed characterizing it, goes 'ancient Israel'. We have not set about *arguing* that the literary 'Israel' is an historical entity, or the 'biblical period' a real epoch; we have from the outset *assumed* it. Literary periodization becomes historical time, literary figures historical figures. Not all the figures, of course: Adam, Noah and maybe even Abraham (for the daring) are eliminated. But taking these figures out makes matters worse: the result is something that is neither historical nor biblical, but a scholarly rationalisation of the literary and the historical. Literary criticism of the Bible became, for generations of students, an historical enterprise [6]

Now let me be clear: I am not as yet saying that the literary Israel must be assumed *a priori* to be unhistorical. What I am saying is that it *is* literary and that it *might* be historical. I am saying that in a well-ordered and critical discipline we might expect a good deal of biblical scholarship to concern itself with discovering how, and then how far, one might set about recovering history from the literature, in this particular case. In other words, one might expect to find a search going on for the historical counterpart of this literary creation. The historicity of the literary 'Israel' ought everywhere to have been firstly a matter of 'whether' and only then, if at all, 'how much'. But this has not been so, with very few exceptions: the procedure adopted by biblical scholarship has instead been to take for granted that what is

6    I am aware that already in the last century biblical scholars reconstructed the history of Israelite *religion* on the basis of a critical reconstruction of the sources. But if they rearranged the furniture, the room was still much the same; the Israel whose religion was being rewritten remained unquestioned. In fairness, it should be remembered that archaeology was not yet able to moderate such judgments. In general, I would suggest that recent biblical scholarship in many respects has yet to be restored to the critical standards of the late 19th century.

literary can be deemed historical, and then to make adjustments or qualifications as these were judged necessary. 'Ancient Israel' was never an *hypothesis*, a possibility to be reconstructed. It was always taken for granted. And the onus of proof has always been on those who doubted the validity of this procedure, who questioned the hypothesis, who were accused of scepticism and hypercriticism, even cynicism. So long as there was 'no reason to doubt that...' there appeared to be every reason to believe, and no obligation to argue, much less prove, was entertained.

Many a reader will perhaps find herself or himself thinking 'but surely, there *was* an historical 'ancient Israel!' The very raising of a doubt might seem absurd, deliberately provocative, programmatically negativistic. Virtually a whole discipline, after all, is predicated on the existence of an 'ancient Israel'. But it is not absurd at all to ask the question, to insist on the search. It only seems absurd because scholars have never opened the question, so that it seems entirely off the agenda. It is the kind of question that threatens with a new paradigm, like the absurd idea that the earth orbited round the sun. The student of the Bible gets the impression that 'ancient Israel' really did exist because she or he reads about it all the time. If one can doubt that the Bible is not history, one can surely not doubt a battalion of professors!

But without benefit of professors students can work the problem out for themselves. The 'Israel' of the biblical literature is at least for the most part quite obviously not an historical entity at all. This much can be deduced from the same scholarly writings that talk about it as if it were. As I have already mentioned, biblical scholars actually know– and write–that most of the 'biblical period' consists not only of unhistorical persons and events, but even of of tracts of time *that do not belong in history at all*! One obvious case is the so-called 'patriarchal period', which has certainly been treated, even fairly recently, as if it were an historical era (even though the proposed datings covered nearly the whole of the second millennium BCE), but is nowadays accepted by the great majority of biblical scholars to be non-existent, to be, as I have put it, a literary construct .(Some scholars may say 'theological construct' which sounds more impressive, but comes to the same thing.) There is now hardly any argument to be found in the pages of scholarly books about when the 'patriarchal period' even *might* have been, had it really existed, because we understand that the setting of the patriarchs[7] is not chronological, but genealogical and ideological. There is simply no point in seeking historical dates for Abraham, Isaac or Jacob, any more than for Enoch or Noah or Terah. The beginnings of the 'biblical period' thus cannot, in fact, be determined in any chronological sense, cannot be translated into any historical periodization. The 'patriarchal age' is an epoch in the literary, biblical story but not in the history of the ancient world.

The same is widely acknowledged, if by a slightly lesser majority, of the 'Exodus' and the 'wilderness period' and a still substantial majority of scholars would probably accept as much for most, if not all, of the 'period' of the 'judges'. The fact that the biblical literature offers a chronology of this last 'period' is beside the point: there is an exact chronology for the lifespans of Adam and Eve, Enoch and Methuselah! Indeed, chronology is almost an indication of *non*-historicity: the creation of a 'judges period' is the most obviously artificial feature of the collection of judge-stories: the sequence of deliverance, judging, apostasy, punishment, is entirely formal, as are the forty-year spells of judging. It is, then, precisely where the story presents itself as most 'history-like' that it is actually most fictional–a point well worth remembering![8]

So neither the 'patriarchal period' nor the 'wilderness period' nor the 'period of the judges' can be transformed into an epoch in the history of Palestine. Fewer and fewer biblical scholars resist this conclusion. Yet the majority of them, while realizing that the story of Israel from Genesis to Judges is not to be treated as history, nonetheless proceed with the rest of the biblical story, from Saul or David onwards on the assumption that at this point in the sequence the obviously literary has now become the obviously historical. Whereas decades ago, histories might begin with the settlement of the Israelites in Palestine, more recent 'Histories of Israel' begin with Saul, or David, or perhaps Omri. However, truncating 'ancient Israel' in this

---

7    These characters are now increasingly called 'ancestors', but their creators referred to them and considered them as 'patriarchs' so I retain the chauvinistic locution. Also 'ancestral age' is not a felicitous term.

8    An excellent treatment of this feature of ancient historiography is given in J. Van Seters, *In Search of History. Historiography in the Ancient World and the Origins of Biblical History*, New Haven and London: Yale University Press, 1983 (to whom I am indebted for more than the title of my book, as will become obvious).

way does not make things easier, but worse. It actually presents a very serious difficulty indeed. Can one really leave out the first part of the literary Israel's history, retain the second part and still proceed to treat it as an historical entity? Certainly not! If the history of 'ancient Israel' is to begin at this point, then it will have to be a very different entity from the literary Israel. For while the literary Israel began life as a family, experienced captivity in Egypt, was delivered from there by its god, made a covenant, received a law and conquered a land divinely donated to it, the reconstructed 'ancient Israel' has none of this, and so has a quite different identity and character. Without such a prehistory, what sort of an 'Israel' are we biblical scholars starting out with? We have only a society that begins life as a nation within Palestine, but no more. Having turned the biblical stories such as those of Abraham, Jacob and Moses into 'traditions' belonging to 'ancient Israel' we have no history on which to hang them, and have to invent a society, usually with some other history, in which they nevertheless make some sense! Or else we ascribe the stories to a later period. In either case, we have no historically-formed identity to this society we have decided nevertheless is an 'Israel'. What is the religion, the culture, of this 'Israel' going to be, then? What, indeed, makes it an 'Israel'? Much as we might pretend that we are presenting a critical reconstruction of the biblical Israel, we are really doing nothing of the kind. By starting at the moment in history that we do, we are abandoning the literary Israel of the Bible, and commencing to write the history of another society. Whether or not it calls itself, or we call it, 'Israel' is really beside the point, because we should not want it confused with the better-known Israel of the Bible. Not, at least, as historians. But are we historians, and do we have motives which pull us in the other direction? Does our discipline after all really not *want* to confuse the two?

Suppose that we accept that our historical society, which we have got into the habit of calling 'ancient Israel', is really not going to be like the biblical Israel, since we have just taken away all the things that gave it its identity. We can then lose interest, having already abandoned the Pentateuch and Joshua and Judges, and decide that we are more interested in what is in the Bible than what is in history. We can revert to being students of literature with no interest in history. Or we can abandon ourselves to our own curiosity, and wonder just who it was that did live in these central Palestinian highlands, and who they thought they were, and where they got their identity from. We could say that we had found a subject to study, and set ourselves a programme of research. But where would be pursue this research? Among the pages of the Bible or among the mountains of Palestine? Having already decided that the Bible is talking about some other society, we had better leave it alone. We shall have to write our hisotry of this unknown population without it, at least in the first instance.

This is not, of course, what biblical scholars do. Rather, they insist that they are still dealing with the Israel of the biblical literature, accept the self-definition of that literary Israel (for which there is no historical explanation, and no need for one) and pretend to do some history. But this is, of course, not history at all: it is a species of *fides quaerens intellectum*. Biblical historians assume an 'ancient Israel' after the manner of the biblical story, and then seek rationalistic explanations for it, instead of asking themselves what is *really* there. Instead of trying to understand what is literary in literary terms, they try to give historical explanations for what are literary problems. Here is where the increasing role of literary criticism in biblical scholarship, however, is making a valuable contribution to historical research, by recognizing and pointing out that the reason why many things are told in the biblical literature, and the way they are told, has virtually everything to do with literary artistry and virtually nothing to do with anything that might have happened.

Certainly, patriarchs and wilderness wanderings and collapsing walls of Jericho belong nowhere in Palestinian history. Whoever is living in the Palestinian highlands around 1000 BCE does not think, look or act like the people the biblical writers have put there. They are literary creations. What, then, shall we make of the rest of the literary Israel? Do we wonder whether we are dealing with a literary construct as we confront Saul, David and Solomon, Jeroboam, Jehu, Hezekiah and Josiah? We have certainly been given good reason to think so in the first two cases.[9] Confidence in the essential historical reliability of the biblical literature is a basis for all 'Histories of Israel', however critical they appear or pretend to be. After all, too

9    Without mentioning the many other works on the figure of David, I refer the reader to D.M. Gunn, *The Story of King David: Genre and Interpretation* (JSOTS, 6), Sheffield: JSOT Press, 1978, and his *The Fate of King Saul: An Interpretation of a Biblical Story* (JSOTS, 14), Sheffield: JSOT Press, 1980.

much caution and one will not be writing a 'History of Israel' at all (which is perhaps where we are heading)!

But concern with history extends well beyond 'Histories of Israel'; it permeates (though decreasingly) the bulk of exegetical work. Consider how many scholarly works deal with the historical dating and context of parts of biblical literature, or with the reconstruction of 'Israel's traditions'. How many commentaries on Isaiah, for instance, concern themselves with what Isaiah thought, what was really happening in his time, what advice he gave to Ahaz and to Hezekiah, what later writers added to his words, when they added them, and so on? Necessary to all such speculation is some kind of historical outline, and not just a sequence of dates but a *Gestalt*, an image of a society in which certain beliefs and certain kinds of behaviour govern. Such a lavishly detailed portrait is impossible to construct from elsewhere. We can learn from the results of archaeology something of the social conditions of Iron Age Palestine. But the literary Israel offers the kind of simplified yet dramatic portrayal that characterizes all great artistic products, those which have the capacity of suspending disbelief. Thus in the case of Isaiah, for instance, we can turn a blind eye to reversing shadows or political advice couched in refined poetry: we can be confident that despite such obviously unlikely embellishments, there is nevertheless a real historical context before us here, an episode in the life of a real 'ancient Israel'.

Consider Amos for moment. We know very little of the social life of the times in which this hero has his words set. We know only that the eponym and implied author of this book criticized certain practices, and we infer from his criticism that certain things were going on. Had he complimented his society instead, we biblical scholars would be viewing that society in diametrically opposite terms, entirely on his say-so, just as most biblical scholarship accepts his say-so now. That is how our discipline operates, and once the literary Israel becomes construed as an historical one that is all we can do. I do not deny that biblical scholars readily doubt the historicity of certain events and figures–the prophetic 'legends' in the books of Kings for instance. The books of Jonah, Esther and Ruth, too, are usually acknowledged as fictional creations. This acknowledgement does not mitigate the charge I am making. It merely makes it harder to understand by what subterranean criteria biblical scholars can distinguish fictions with real historical settings from historical accounts. It is impossible to discern any grounds for deciding that on the one hand the Joseph story is not historical, while on the other hand the accounts of the life and times of David or Ezra are.

The fact is, then, that our 'ancient Israel' is a not the biblical literary entity, nor an historical one. It is a scholarly creation deemed essential to the pursuit of biblical studies, and it has come about by the simple but erroneous step of lifting one kind of thing out of a text and setting it down somewhere else. It owes nearly everything to Bible reading, nothing to critical reflection, and very little indeed to historical research. It looks very much like the procedure of a discipline motivated by theology and religious sentiment, not critical scholarship. But let us return to this theme a little later in the chapter.

### *What society has 'ancient Israel' displaced?*

Exporting a literary construct and dumping it into Iron Age Palestine has succeeded in creating a 'history of ancient Israel'. But it has also interfered with the real history of Palestine, which now has a cuckoo in its nest. For of course, as I remarked earlier, there *was* a population of Iron Age Palestine, including a kingdom called Israel, and real people lived there, real kings ruled, real wars took place and real transportations, in and out, were practised by conquering armies and sovereigns. *These* are the people and societies whose relics archaeologists discover whenever they dig for 'ancient Israel'. If it is clear that biblical scholars are not writing *their* history, who will write it? Who will write the history of a people whose real character has been obliterated by a literary construct? If what I am saying is right, biblical scholarship is guilty of a retrojective imperialism, which displaces an otherwise unknown and uncared-for population in the interests of an ideological construct.

Let me illustrate this point. Assume that two different scholars are set a task, one of writing a history of the population of central Palestine in the Iron Age and the other of writing the history of ancient Israel. Would each understand that the two of them were being set the same task? Would they set about it the same way? Would they use the same sources? Would they produce the same result? My guess is that they would do different things. The former would go to primarily archaeological data, and might use the biblical data sparingly and cautiously, while the latter would use the biblical literature and use archaeology in a supportive role.[10] In each case the choice of material would be largely compelled by the nature of the task. One would begin by finding out what *was* the population of central Palestine, where they came from, the languages they spoke, their religions, culture and so on. The other would not. But, to go by the evidence, she or he, if a biblical scholar, would not think there were any difference between 'ancient Israel' and the population of Iron Age central Palestine. Certainly, no biblical scholar has ever explicated that distinction. If the population of central Palestine *is* 'ancient Israel', then we can use the terms interchangeably. But then we would have to ask why our two scholars are proceeding in different ways to describe the same thing. If there is a *difference* between the two, then we have to ask what it is, and how an archaeologist can tell the two apart. Can the distinction be made independently of the biblical story? Can we show, independently of the biblical literature, that what must be happening in Palestine in the Iron Age is the history of an 'ancient Israel'?

*Double vision*

Now we come to an issue which apparently complicates the rather neat dichotomy I have been imposing, and which the alert reader will already have anticipated. The literary Israel whose historical counterpart I am casting into doubt presents us with several figures, places and events which we happen to know belong to the history of Palestine. How shall I account for the presence of such history in the biblical construct if I wish to insist on a separation of the two? For many a biblical scholar, these common elements afford a pretext–some would say, provide evidence–for turning the literary Israel into an historical one. Ahab and Jehu, for example, are known to us from Assyrian inscriptions as well as from biblical writings; Sennacherib's siege of Jerusalem (of which 2 Kings and Isaiah write) is graphically and textually depicted in Assyrian records and reliefs, and names

10  I wonder how many Egyptologists would begin their exploration of ancient Egypt by reading Manetho, or Assyriologists by reading Berossus, or ancient historians by reading Herodotus. The question is not, of course, whether or not literary sources contain historical clues, but whether a literary text from a later period is the right place to get your basic premises from.

Hezekiah of Judah. The Lachish ostraca document the Babylonian invasion of the Shephelah and the Judaean highlands. We can read from a Babylonian text of that Jehoiachin (he of 2 Kings) was given rations at the Babylonian court. Yes, indeed: the biblical Israel shares characters and events with the historical populations of Palestine. There are overlaps in respect of particular persons, and even particular events. Shall we say 'archaeology confirms the Bible!'?

I might try to answer this by appealing to Shakespeare's character 'Julius Caesar' or Malory's 'King Arthur'. From such examples I could argue that it is easy to avoid confusing the Caesar of history with the Caesar of the Elizabethan stage. I could also concede that if we allow that the presence of historical persons, events and places suggests the historicity of a literary work, then in fairness the opposite should also apply, and non-appearance of known historical entities should tell against historicity. Both arguments are in fact silly. One cannot say that Dickens's London is more remote from history than a Hollywood film about Jack the Ripper, simply because the latter contains an historical character. It is well known that authentic geographical settings and genuine chronological settings do not of themselves guarantee the historicity of anything described as happening there (e.g. *A Tale of Two Cities*). The existence of common names, places and events between an historical construct and a literary one does not necessarily make the literary construct historical.

But these are points of general principle. A fuller explanation can be offered by taking a concrete example of such a case. Let us consider the siege of Jerusalem by Sennacherib in c. 701 BCE, which is, as most students of the Bible know, reported by Assyrian inscriptions and a biblical story.[11] In the Assyrian account, Sennacherib devastated Judah, destroying 46 cities, driving out more than 200,000 people, giving Hezekiah's towns to others, and finally, without capturing Jerusalem, exacting from Hezekiah a much bigger tribute than had originally been withheld. The biblical story has Hezekiah making a very large payment to Sennacherib before the siege (presumably to forestall it). Despite this, the siege was conducted but ended in defeat for Sennacherib, who lost 185,000 of his troops to an angel. Now the accounts are not wildly dissimilar, and they permit

---

11   For the Assyrian account, see *ANET*, pp. 287-88; for the biblical account, 2 Kings 18.13–19.37; Isa. 36–37.

us to make a reasonable guess that the Assyrians devastated Judah, that Jerusalem was not captured, and that Hezekiah paid a huge tribute.

So let us ask why they are different. The reason is partly because neither account is interested in the mere event. The discrepancy over the occasion of the payment is not an accidental one: the biblical account implies treachery on Sennacherib's part, while Sennacherib's account implies that Hezekiah only paid up when he was about to lose the one city that he had left. If we take in a slightly wider vista, we can see that Sennacherib's account belongs with a number of other similar texts which serve the vanity of the Assyrian monarchs, sustain the loyalty and cohesion of the Assyrian nation, and probably intend to cow would-be rebels into renouncing thoughts of rebellion. Hezekiah is referred to as merely 'the Judaean'. The biblical story (and actually the two versions of it do not exactly agree) is designed to show that Yahweh can and will rescue his chosen city. Indeed, it makes no further reference to an Assyrian yoke, implying, it seems, that the deliverance from the Assyrians was permanent.

Now, I am not really interested in contrasting the biblical and Assyrian accounts. It can be agreed that there is an event here and that both sources refer to it in some way. The issue we are dealing with is the history of 'ancient Israel' compared with the history of ancient Palestine. The point I have been making so far is that 'ancient Israel' is a literary construct, but not that fortunes of this 'ancient Israel' are entirely imaginary. The biblical story is based on something that happened (as is the Assyrian story), but *to whom* did it happen? What happened in the history of Palestine was this: a vassal king of Judah rebelled against his Assyrian overlord, was severely punished both by losing virtually all of his kingdom except Jerusalem and by paying an enormous tribute. Afterwards he remained a vassal of Assyria, without the power of rebellion (too small, too poor). Now, what happened to 'ancient Israel'? A victory of the god of Israel, Yahweh, defender of Zion and his chosen Davidic dynasty over the Assyrian king, which left Judah ever after free of Assyrian control (for it is never again referred to).[12] Can we really say that there are not two

---

12   A superb treatment of this and related topics was given by E. Ben Zvi in a paper 'History and Prophetic Texts', delivered at the 1991 Annual SBL Meeting. I am grateful to him for making a copy of his text available to me. There is, of course, an allusion to Assyrian hegemony at a latyer period in 2 Chron. 33.11, which states that military officials of the king of Assyria took Manasseh to Babylon, as a result of

different stories here, and that these stories belong to two different histories. (We could add the Assyrian story as a third). To whom did this happen? It happened to the literary Israel, and it happened to an historical king of Judah. I do not wish to say that it happened to 'ancient Israel', for there is no such event to be reconstructed. It would be an event that neither Sennacherib nor the books of Kings and Isaiah record. So much, then, for the argument that events in the history of the biblical Israel which are echoed elsewhere prove the existence of an 'ancient Israel'; they merely prove that it happened to *someone*. The elements in the biblical account which differ from those recorded by Sennacherib are not incidental nor reducible to 'interpretation'. They are all tightly bound up with the characterization of the hero as 'Israel' (just as Sennacherib's is bound up with his own glorification). Jerusalem in the biblical story was delivered, and by its deity, because it was the one legitimate sanctuary of 'ancient Israel', because it had a Davidic king, recipient of a dynastic promise from Yahweh the 'holy one of Israel' The events are described as they are because Israel is involved. And to this Israel happen things that as an historian I do not accept happen in history here or anywhere else. Why the biblical story is as it is can in the last analysis be explained only if we recognize that it is not simply giving us a different version of an historical event, but is telling us a story of something that is not historical. To return to an earlier analogy, Brutus, in Shakespeare's *Julius Caesar* kills his friend, makes his speech, and meets his death at the hands of Antony because Shakespeare's Brutus is a dramatic figure, of the tragic kind who, though honourable, must die. Brutus does what he does in this play because of the play's own dramatic logic. Whatever any historical Brutus may or may not have done does not either explain this character's actions nor does it make Shakespeare's character into an historical one.

This part of my argument, then, can be concluded by reiterating first of all what is important to bear in mind: that I am not at all pretending that events and characters in the story of either the biblical Israel or the scholarly 'ancient Israel' do not have historical counterparts. This in turn must imply that the creators of this literary

which he repented; but Chronicles implies that the Assyrians were brought in specifically for the purpose of teaching Manasseh a lesson, not that they were permanent suzerains. The historicity of this episode is also quite strenuously debated.

construct had some knowledge of events in the history of Palestine (as did Shakespeare of Roman history, through his reading of Plutarch). It does not imply that they therefore intended to narrate the event in a way which accurately described it (if indeed they knew how to do that), nor that their 'Israel' is an historical entity any more than their Abraham, Joseph, Joshua or Samson. The error of assuming that the presence of historical elements in the biblical story is evidence of the historicity of 'ancient Israel' needs to be recognized for what it is. This sort of naivety will not do for historical research, if we are serious about that.

### *Tail chasing*

Another factor in the misconstrual of 'ancient Israel' by biblical scholars is an argument that has somehow developed (we shall see why presently) that the originators of the biblical literature lived within the period which that literature itself narrates. At first sight, and to an outsider, this idea might seem implausible, but students of biblical criticism quickly assimilate this as a basic presupposition. Had it been acknowledged, of course, that the biblical construct of 'Israel' emanated from a different society than the one depicted in the biblical literature, say from the inhabitants of Yehud in the fifth century BCE and onwards, the sort of argument I am trying to make (at some length) would have been relatively easy, and probably unnecessary. A literary artifact of some centuries later than what it purports to describe would not have been so readily mistaken as an historical construct, and at the very least would have no priority over artifactual and inscriptional data from the Iron Age. Historical research into the literary construct would have focussed on this later period of composition, and an entirely new set of methods and assumptions for understanding the Bible might have evolved. But this did not happen, or has not happened yet. So far, historical research by biblical scholars has taken a different route. The route is a circular one, and its stages can be represented more or less as follows:

1. The biblical writers, when writing about the past, were obviously both informed about it and often concerned to report it accurately to their readers. A concern with the truth of the past can be assumed. Therefore, where the literary history is plausible, or where it encounters no insuperable

objections, it should be accorded the status of historical fact. The argument is occasionally expressed that the readers of these stories would be sufficiently knowledgeable (by tradition?) of their past to discourage wholesale invention.

2. Much of the literature is itself assigned to quite specific settings within that story (e.g. the prophetic books, dated to the reigns of kings of Israel and Judah).[13] If the biblical literature is generally correct in its historical portrait, then these datings may also be relied upon.

3. Even where the various parts of the biblical literature do not date themselves within the history of its 'Israel' we are given a precise enough account in general to enable plausible connections can be made, such as Deuteronomy with the time of Josiah, or (as formerly) the Yahwist with the time of David or Solomon, Psalms with a Jerusalem cult. Thus, where a plausible context in the literary history can be found for a biblical writing, that setting may be posited, and as a result there will be *mutual confirmation*, by the literature of the setting, and by the setting of the literature. For example, the Yahwist's setting in the court of Solomon tells us about the character of that monarchy and the character of that monarchy explains the writing of this story.

4. Where the writer ('redactor') of the biblical literature is recognized as having been removed in time from the events he[14] describes or persons whose words he reports (e.g. when an account of the history of 'Israel' stretches over a long period of time), he must be presumed to rely on sources or traditions close to the events. Hence even when the literary source is late, its contents will nearly always have their point of origin in the time of which they speak. The likelihood of a

13 Obviously, a good deal of the literature is not historiographical in form. However, what is now the Pentateuch and Former Prophets, plus Ezra, Nehemiah and Chronicles belong to this genre while the Major Prophets, most of the Minor Prophets, Ruth, Daniel, Esther posit concrete historical settings. (In the case of most of the remainder, such as it is, biblical scholarship has been keen to secure an historical background–I think especially of Psalms.)

14 I use the masculine form deliberately, since I believe that the writers of the literature should be construed, at least collectively, as a male society (and a particular one). I do not rule out the possibility of literature originating with women, either as individuals or collectively.

writer inventing something should generally be discounted in
favour of a tradition, since traditions allow us a vague
connection with 'history' (which does not have to be exact)
and can themselves be accorded some value as historical
statements of the 'faith' of 'Israel' (and this will serve the
theologian almost as well as history).

Each one of these assertions can be encountered, in one form or
another in secondary literature. But it is the underlying logic which
requires attention rather than these (dubious) assertions themselves.
That logic is circular. The assumption that the literary construct is an
historical one is made to confirm itself. Historical criticism (so-called)
of the inferred sources and traditions seeks to locate these in that
literary-cum-historical construct. The placement of sources and
traditions in this way can then be used to embellish the literary
account itself. This circular process *places the composition of the
literature within the period of which the literature itself speaks.* This
is precisely how the period to which the biblical literature refers
becomes also the time of composition, the 'biblical period', and the
biblical literature, taken as a whole, becomes a *contemporary witness
to its own construct*, reinforcing the initial assumption of a real
historical construct and giving impetus to an entire pseudo-scholarly
exercise in fitting the literature into a sequence of contexts which it
has itself furnished! If either the historicity of the biblical construct or
the actual date of composition of its literature were to be verified
independently of each other, the circle could be broken. But the
methodological need has virtually never been seen, and so the
circularity has continued to characterize an entire discipline–and
indeed render it invalid.

The panoply of historical-critical tools and methods used by biblical
scholars relies for the most part on this basic circularity. Once it is
taken for granted that that the biblical literature is largely an Iron Age
product,[15] volumes such as *Ancient Near Eastern Texts Relating to the
Old Testament*,[16] can be taken to convey the message that not only do

15   The use of deliberately different terminology is important as a way of
critically distancing the language of the historian from that either borrowed from the
bible or dependent on its own concepts: by 'Iron Age' I mean what biblical scholars
refer to by 'pre-exilic'; equally, what I mean by 'Persian' is commonly called 'post-
exilic'.

16   J. Pritchard (ed.), *Ancient Near Eastern Texts Relating to the Old Testament*,

these texts relate to the biblical *content* but also to the *forms* that the biblical literature employs. Form-criticism, with its focus on smaller units, attempts to connect these constituent units (for the most part) with *Sitze im Leben* from the period of Iron Age Palestinian society– *Sitze* depicted in, or inferred from, the biblical literature, of course, and not reconstructed from artifactual data. Moreover, by its concentration on these smaller units rather than the larger compositional units, form-criticism has ignored the possible significance for dating, origin and function of the biblical literature of the larger genres which constitute the shape of the biblical narrative. Form-criticism largely and perhaps conveniently forgets that meaning, structure, and social setting are also dimensions of these larger compositions, and in its obsession with the 'original' forms does not direct its methods to the elucidation of the larger (and less hypothetical) units. One of the major larger genres of the biblical literature is historiography, and yet this genre, without parallel in the 'Ancient Near Eastern' Literature has hardly attracted until recently a fraction of the structural, rhetorical and comparative analysis of other smaller *Gattungen*.[17] For recognition of the integrity of larger compositional units we have to thank, for the most part, the work of literary biblical scholars in recent years, although few of them were interested in the historical context of these more extended compositions.[18]

Redaction-critics and tradition-historians do not form exceptions to this generalization. Each of these methods, it seems to me, is practised within the circle. The term 'redaction' emphasizes the existence of earlier materials which are worked over, while 'tradition' assumes a process of retelling, and thus the pre-existence of material before its writing down by the author. In each case the recognition of an original creative process preceding by several stages and by a long span of time the actual creation of the literary work (however identified) was generated by assumption rather than critically established. In assigning contexts for the composition of biblical

Princeton: Princeton University Press, 3rd ed., 1969.

17    A point made by J. Van Seters, *In Search of History*.

18    As explained by K.W. Whitelam, 'Between History and Literature: The Social Production of Israel's Traditions of Origin', *SJOT* 2 (1991), pp. 60-74. J. Muilenburg's famous essay on rhetorical criticism ('Form Criticism and Beyond', *JBL* 88 [1969], pp. 1-18) had already attacked form-criticism along these lines.

literature which are furnished by the literature itself, biblical scholarship is, at least methodologically speaking, chasing its own tail. The critical methods of biblical scholarship, or at least the way in which they are practised, are in conspiracy with the assumption of an 'ancient Israel' which wrote scrolls about itself.

## Common Sense and Credulity

To the charge of circularity which forms, as I see it, the methodological heart of biblical historical criticism, needs to be added that of credulity. The two examples I am about to offer illustrate the way in which biblical data come to inform scholarly hypotheses without the intervention of common sense.

The first of these is also a brilliant example of circularity: the 'Josianic reform'. According to 2 Kings 22–23 a 'book of the covenant' was discovered in the Temple, which discovery led to a royal reform. The details of the reform suggest that the king was following the requirements of the book of Deuteronomy or some form of it. This reform has long been a linchpin of biblical history, for upon it much of the scholarly reconstruction of the history of 'Israelite' literature depends. Let us first remind ourselves that the *only* evidence for such a reform is the biblical story itself. Then let us recall where the story occurs, namely in a book whose ideology seems to be influenced by, or at least to lie very close to, that of the book of Deuteronomy. The argument of this book (2 Kings) is that if the principles of Deuteronomy (for so they are) had been observed by 'Israel' then the kingdom of Judah would not, like its counterpart over a century earlier, have come to an end. Thus, a piece of writing which is ideologically, and in some places linguistically, close to the book of Deuteronomy claims that a law book, which it describes in a way which makes it look very like Deuteronomy, was once upon a time discovered by a king and implemented (although the king was conveniently killed and the reform overturned). Here we have before us an unverified attempt to give Deuteronomy some antique authority and to argue that its contents are appropriate for implementation in a political body. How much credence shall we biblical critics give to such a story? What might a lawyer make of it? A juror? An ordinary person? Hardly reliable testimony; at least it needs some support before we can base any conclusions upon it. But scarcely a biblical scholar has ever entertained the thought (at least in print) that this story might just be a convenient legend, that maybe no such reform took place. But suppose we do suspend our disbelief and take the story on trust. Is it likely, then, that we can imagine the contents of Deuteronomy being implemented by a king? Deuteronomy has very little indeed to say about the responsibilities and powers of kings–very strange for any such document in the Iron Age, when virtually all authority was assumed by the crown–and the supreme powers of the king, administration of justice and waging of war are assigned to others (elders, priests). The monarch is expected, according to Deuteronomy, to rule by a book. Well, one cannot declare it impossible that a king of Judah did such a thing; we can only say that it is an unlikely supposition. Even were the king himself disposed to such a virtual abdication, there will have been many around him who, owing their power to the institution of monarchy, would have prevented any such rash abandon. What is a *reasonable* verdict on an implausible story from a highly partial witness? The 'reform of Josiah' is bound to be regarded as a pious legend, just about possible, perhaps, but extremely improbable.

Now this verdict has some serious consequences. It renders the dating of Deuteronomy itself uncertain, and with the freeing of Deuteronomy from its place a lot of other scholarly hypotheses are dislodged too, including the process of formation of the Pentateuch, of the book of Jeremiah and the dating of the so-called 'Deuteronomistic history'. It also removes a favourite epoch of tradition- and redaction-critics, for Josianic redactions and reinterpretations have bred at an impressive rate in recent years. To build so much upon an unjustified gesture of credulity is irresponsible, and I hope it illustrates dramatically the fragility of a good deal of biblical historical scholarship.

A second example illustrates especially how biblical scholars, in their fondness for the literary construct, can get themselves into a way of thinking that fits literature better than it does history. I am thinking of the so-called 'exile'. An historical deportation from Judah (deportation being a very common experience in those days) and a transportation of population out of Babylonia into Judah several decades later can certainly be accepted as historically probable. In that sense there is no doubting an overlap between the experiences of the population of early sixth century Judah and the biblical Israel. But the 'exile' of the biblical literature and of biblical scholarship is no mere deportation. The biblical literature presents us with an 'exile' of most of the population to Babylonia, followed by an emptying of the land, an emptiness also evaluated as a 'sabbath rest' for the land.[19] The result is that the 'exiles' who then return constitute all of 'Israel' and have a land to themselves (apart, perhaps, from alien settlers?). As far as the 'exile' itself is concerned, the biblical literature presents it both as a punishment and then also as a mercy: it punishes the wicked nation and then preserves it intact ready for reinstallation in the land promised to it. *This* is the 'exile' and as such it is an ideological and not a historical construct, though an ideologically contradictory one, as I have remarked. It is also in contradiction with the function and effect of deportation as we know this from the ancient Near East, where it was extremely common.The physical circumstances are not different from the deportations, transportations and resettlements that were a regular part of life, but the 'exile' is in a way a denial of the policy of deportation, more precisely a defiance of it. Historically, deportations are intended to destroy nationality, while the biblical 'exile' is a means of preserving it.

Biblical scholarship, true to the procedure which characterizes it, has taken the biblical 'exile' as an historical description, preservation and all, and then developed its own historical construct, a period during which many prophetic books were redacted, the Deuteronomistic history was edited, the Priestly writings encoded, the poems of 'Second Isaiah' composed, and often much else. Of this period we *actually* know next to nothing. We have preserved for us a note of rations for Jehoiachin of Judah, we have the Murashu archives, showing (perhaps) many prosperous Jews later running businesses in Babylonia. We know that centuries later there is a Babylonian Jewish community. But the idea that the authentic 'Israel' was preserved by deportees and replanted in Palestine several decades later by their grandchildren is a fairly suspicious piece of ideology on the part of the biblical writers and even more dubious speculation on the part of biblical scholars. All that the biblical ideology of 'exile' proves is that the rulers and writers of the Persian province of Yehud who came (in large measure, at least) from Babylonia claimed that

19   For an analysis of this ideology, see R.P. Carroll, 'Textual Strategies and Ideology in the Second Temple Period', in P.R. Davies (ed.) *Second Temple Studies* (JSOTS, 117), Sheffield: JSOT Presss, 1991, pp. 108-124.

they were the legitimate judges of what was right–that they could rule, legislate, and be priests, because they had brought the ancient law and preserved the authentic priesthood. Underlying these rights, of course, is the fundamental right to interpret history! They seem to have exercised these claims over biblical scholarship as well, which has mostly renounced its duty to ask whether these claims are true simply because they are pressed, and pressed in the Bible.

If we set aside for a moment the 'exile', and reflect on what we know or may reasonably surmise about deportations, we find ourselves somewhat incredulous about the plausibility not so much of the contradictory biblical picture, but of the scholarly reconstruction, which obliges us to picture deportees carrying much of their (presumed) traditional literature with them, presumably in scrolls. Now, the point of deportation, whether as punishment or as resource management (as it frequently was) is to break a link between deportees and their homeland, and the idea of exiled priests (or administrators) carrying bundles of scrolls is a curious one. Again, the deported community is depicted as having been deliberated settled in such a way as to reconstitute their native culture on foreign soil. This would be unusual, and there is no evidence outside the biblical story for this state of affairs. It is not impossible, but equally there is no reason to think it happened. Even the biblical story suggests that these 'exiles' did not return in large numbers, nor even in moderate numbers, and not without need for persuasion, so that the idea of a compact community nurturing memories of home is not borne out even in biblical scholarship's primary source! According to the biblical story itself, those who did 'return' to Judah failed to build the Temple immediately and seem initially to have had little idea of what they were doing. In short, the biblical account needs to be recognized as ideological and inconsistent, and the scholarly hypotheses about it have no basis whatsoever. The biblical, literary Israel suffered exile, the population of the Palestinian kingdom of Judah suffered deportation (of an extent we do not know), while biblical scholarship has invented a glorious epoch of creativity for its own construct, 'ancient Israel' which if anything is even less historically plausible than the biblical picture. It is pretty silly to assign the composition of large tracts of the biblical literature to a deportation,[20] but it is a very

---

20   C.C. Torrey's famous critique of 1910 ('The Exile and the Restoration', in *Ezra Studies*, reprinted New York, Ktav, 1970, pp. 285-340) has frequently been

*romantic* idea, and one worthy of the biblical writers had they thought of it. And it is necessitated in a way by the corner into which biblical scholarship has pinned itself. It has to acknowledge that the biblical literature is almost entirely later than the 'pre-exilic' period, but by making it exilic it can pretend that what is being preserved is the old 'pre-exilic' culture and can demonstrate a reason for its preservation— severance from the land and the need to reflect upon the just and divine punishment for its past sins. The characterization of this time as one of reflection and repentance and even religious reform points us to the essentially theological or religious nature of much of biblical scholarship.

## 'Ancient Israel' as a theological construct

It is not uncommon to find 'ancient Israel' in scholarly textbooks referred to as a 'community', and this characterization is based on the premise that 'ancient Israel' produced the Bible. Thus, any biblical idea can be automatically ascribed to 'ancient Israel', and the sum total of these ideas can be taken to comprise its 'faith' or 'view' or 'religion'. Now, societies do not write literature, at least not directly. It is individuals, members of classes, or schools *within a society* which actually produce literature in the ancient Near East, and literature is produced for specific reasons and under specific socio-economic and political conditions: societies as a whole do not have a monolithic ideology ('faith'). The world of the king is not necessarily that of the scribe, nor the scribe's that of the priest, nor the merchant's that of the potter nor the potter's that of the peasant. From what we know of ancient societies, such groups will have had different, sometimes competing interests (whether or not articulated), and different *Weltanschauungen*. To ascribe authorship of the biblical literature to 'ancient Israel', then, is misleading. We do, of course, commonly use such shorthand ways of speaking, as when we believe that to the British people, for instance, can be ascribed the policies of its government (which for most of the time, God forbid, since

ridiculed, and usually misrepresented but its arguments not yet refuted. Morton Smith's excellent *Palestinian Parties and Politics That Shaped the Old Testament*, so much in the spirit of Torrey, nevertheless depends too much on the historical events Smith reconstructs from the 'restoration' to be able to endorse Torrey's work, as he of all people might have been expected to.

governments have less scope for moral freedom). But when it comes to the serious matter of recognizing a social entity through its writings, the concept of 'ancient Israel' (or for that matter any ancient society), as an *author* is a nonsense. One cannot interchange the terms 'community' and 'society' as is so frequently done in this case. Yet 'ancient Israel' has become synonymous with the Old Testament itself,[21] and is referred to often as a 'community of faith'. Indeed, it also doubles as the 'people of God' in some more blatantly theological 'scholarship', as if that were not true, *mutatis mutandis*, of any nation with a national deity (though their 'gods' are spelt with lower case letters). The Canaanites and Moabites and Assyrians are not spoken of as communities, and the Moabite stone does not express the faith of 'ancient Moab', even though its ideology is very close to the parts of the biblical one. There is something special about 'ancient Israel' in this regard, and it has less to do with history and more with ecclesiology. In this last section, I want to address the problem of why biblical scholarship is so lacking in the instincts of historical research and so amenable to the biblical ideology. The authors of the biblical literary Israel will be the object of our search somewhat later. At the moment we can tackle the easier task of identifying the authors of the

---

21    There is surely no need to itemize literature of this kind, and it is somewhat invidious to select examples. However, from a random selection of a single bookshelf in a colleague's room, I note the following: H-J. Kraus's *Worship in Israel* (ET Oxford: Blackwell, 1965), which opens with a chapter subtitled 'Historical Survey of the Study of Old Testament Worship', commencing with the statement  'The Christian Church in every age has approached Old Testament worship...' (p.1); on p. 24 we read, still, 'The account of the history of Old Testament worship which follows....The main Israelite festivals are first examined.....' The same equation (this time Bible=Israel) is true of Y. Kaufmann's *The Religion of Israel* (ET Chicago: University of Chicago Press, 1960). More recently, see J. K. Kuntz's *The People of Ancient Israel. An Introduction to Old Testament Literature, History and Thought*, New York: Harper & Row, 1974; R.W. Klein, *Israel in Exile. A Theological Interpretation*, Philadelphia, 1979. Exactly the same equation is happily made in such books as E.W. Nicholson, *God and His People. Covenant and Theology in the Old Testament*, Oxford: Clarendon Press, 1986, which concludes with a chapter on 'The Covenant and the Distinctiveness of Israel's Faith.' All of these books should be considered as typical examples of biblical scholarship, and I intend no particular critique of them as individual achievements. On the other hand, a book such as P.D. Hanson's *The People Called. The Growth of Community in the Bible*, San Francisco: Harper and Row, 1986, is a historically worthless exercise in theological homiletics.

scholarly construct 'ancient Israel' and their own ideology.

Two obvious deductions are that these people are scholars and also theologians. Biblical scholarship is viewed by most of its practitioners, and by nearly all non-practitioners, as a theological discipline. The common habitat of the subject is the seminary or the theological department of a college or University. In secondary schools, it is taught in Religious Education and rarely in literature classes. The majority of biblical scholars are Christians and many of these are clergy. The 'ancient Israel' to which biblical scholarship is in the habit of referring is a miraculously homogeneous entity, an embryonic church, thinking religiously, sinning but ultimately justified by its 'faith' in God (this God being also the God of the scholars, of course). However, the problem with biblical scholarship is not really at root the proclivities of its individual practitioners, since many or most of these are, besides Christian believers, also intelligent critical thinkers, while a small minority of biblical scholars do not have a Christian (or Jewish) belief at all. It has not been my wish in this argument to criticize individual scholars, deserving though some are of it. Nor, to be frank, do I pretend to acquit myself from blame. My quarrel is not with my fellow-travellers but with the structure of the discipline which binds us together in what I see as a mistaken enterprise.

For the disease inflicting biblical scholarship is systemic, and not ultimately the fault of any of biblical scholars, however complicit most of them are in its misguided agenda. It is actually very hard to indulge in what passes for biblical scholarship without accepting a good deal of what a religious sceptic might want to question. We speak, for instance, of 'prophetic preaching,' of 'Israel's faith', of 'God', and we generally endorse what the biblical heroes write and do; we do not suggest Jeremiah is a quisling, that Ezekiel is a pornographic or schizophrenic bigot or that Amos has nothing to offer the downcast of society except *Schadenfreude*. Any one of these reactions could well be justified if the characters were non-Biblical. Our own scholarly traditions, though, impel us to affirm what the Bible says. How often will one find a commentary on a biblical book that deplores its contents? More recent forms of biblical study such as feminist and liberation hermeneutics are offering a partial challenge to what tends otherwise to be an obsequious and credulous pseudo-discipline. But even here one finds an instinct to 'redeem the Bible' for women and for the oppressed; for every feminist who is prepared to accuse the biblical literature of an unacceptable ideology, there are a host of those willing to plead mitigation, offer character references or argue for acquittal.

As a consequence, 'ancient Israel', which is one of the fundamental projects of this pseudo-scholarship, will live on, imaginary as it ever was, but now enshrined in the hearts of biblical theologians. So long as the discipline remains theological, much of what has been said in this chapter will be unacceptable. There will be no search for the history that no one thinks is missing; instead, the great reluctance will persist to look hard for 'ancient Israel' in the life of Iron Age Palestine, for fear that it might not be there, that an unrecognizable ancient Palestinian kingdom might be all that there is. The lack of a search tells us little about what is missing in history, but a lot about the discipline which takes so much for granted, believes so readily,[22] and which in the end, in my view, fails to take the reality of history seriously because it is looking for something that is its own reflection. The history of Iron Age Palestine will be made to conform to the biblical and the biblical-scholarly prejudices and not vice-versa.

I have expressed myself somewhat savagely, and in over-general terms. In part, I feel this necessary in view of the inordinate complacency of the discipline. Nevertheless, I hope to justify, at least in good measure, the criticisms I have made, and to show that a search for the nature and the source of the biblical Israel might provide a valuable working agenda for the next generation of historical biblical research. Anyone familiar with the range of current scholarship will know that the gap between the biblical Israel and the history of Palestine.is widening, and that new scholarly constructs are in the process of emerging. I do not imagine that the theological agenda will ever wane, nor is there any reason why theology should not continue

---

22   There may be a reason for the deification of credulity and the abomination of scepticism. In the language of Christianity, believing is good and doubting is bad (as Luther, for one, would never have had it!). To disbelieve the historicity of the biblical record is sometimes necessary (though the *religious* value of the disbelieved account should always be stressed); but disbelieving should never be made into a systematic approach. Scepticism smacks of irreligiosity, and in biblical studies carries a pejorative tone, at least when applied to the biblical data. Thus the biblical account of history, however, should always be believed until and unless there are grounds for doubting it. If 'scepticism' is deemed too slight, 'cynicism' may be employed, which implies that if one has no faith in what the biblical record says, one has no faith in anything.

to have an interest in biblical scholarship or vice-versa. But it cannot be acceptable that this view monopolizes the discipline to the extent that it dictates an entirely unacceptable way of doing historical research. It might even be better to return to the doctrine of 'salvation history' for theology which at least does not subscribe to the pretence that it has anything to do with real historical research.

Chapter Three

DEFINING THE BIBLICAL ISRAEL

In this chapter I want to backtrack a step. 'Ancient Israel' is based, I have argued, on a biblical, literary construct, which is then made into an historical one. I have argued that this transformation is hardly ever explicit. Among the voluminous secondary literature dealing with 'ancient Israel', including every 'History of Israel', 'Religion of Israel', dictionary entry, or even in the recent debate about the origins of 'Israel', one finds remarkably little consideration of what the term 'Israel' might mean when used by an historian, whether a political, ethnic, or a religious group, or all three.[1] The premise of biblical scholarship seems to be that we may speak of 'Israel' without further definition–in other words, that we know what it is that we are talking about, and we need only to tell its story in a way appropriate to modern canons of historical scholarship. 'Israel', or 'Ancient Israel', is seen to need fuller *description*, but there is no *a priori* doubt about its *essence*. It is axiomatic that the question of *essence* has already been taken care of by the biblical literature. 'Israel' is a given, and we can discuss 'its' history and 'its' religion and 'its' social institutions: we do not need to begin with a critical analysis of what 'it' actually is, or was.

But the argument I shall make in this chapter is that the biblical Israel is such a diverse, confusing and even contradictory notion, when reconstructed historically, that there should never be–indeed, there really *can* never properly be the kind of transference I have suggested. In brief, biblical Israel is a *problem*, and not a datum,

1    I must single out one exception: J.M. Miller and J.H. Hayes, *A History of Ancient Israel and Judah*, Philadelphia: Westminster, 1986, the very title of which shows the definition in question to be political, and hence the term 'Israel' to be reserved for the Samarian state. This usage is, of course, a biblical one, and in other respects the Miller–Hayes treatment depends heavily on the data supplied for the biblical 'Israel'.

when one engages in historical research. Indeed, it is well known that 'Israel' is used in quite a fluid way in the biblical literature. In his 1962 monograph on the definition of Israel, A.R. Hulst[2] concluded that the following uses can be detailed:

1.   the name of the ancestor Jacob
2.   the name of the sacral league of tribes
3.   the name of a united kingdom whose capital was Jerusalem
4.   the name of one of the kingdoms into which that kingdom was subsequently 'divided', i.e. the 'northern kingdom'
5.   after 722 as another name for Judah
6.   after the exile as a name for the *Gemeente (Gemeinde)*, the socio-religious community within the province of Yehud
7.   as the name of a group within this community, the laity (as distinct from 'Aaron').

J.H. Hayes[3] has added to these three more

8.   a name for descendants of Jacob/Israel
9.   a pre-monarchic tribal grouping in Ephraim
10.  adherents of various forms of Hebrew and Old Testament religion

There are thus at least ten senses to be distinguished within the biblical literature itself–and yet 'distinguished' is precisely what they are not when it comes to historical presupposition. The biblical literature in most cases makes no explicit distinctions, and biblical scholars rarely make it clear in which of the biblical senses they employ the term. However, the point is not simply that the reader of the Bible ought to know at any point which 'Israel' is being read about, nor even that the scholar ought always to make clear in which sense (s)he means it to be understood. No: it is not a matter of picking the definition that is wanted at any one time. Rather, it has first to be asked *what kind of a term this is*, which is both so fundamental to the

2    A.R. Hulst, *Wat betekent de naam ISRAEL in het Oude Testament?*, 's-Gravenhaag, 1962. See also G.A. Danell, *Studies in the Name Israel in the Old Testament*, Uppsala, 1945; R. Albertz, C. Thoma & H. Hübner, 'Israel I-III', *Theologische Realenzyklopädie* 16, Berlin: De Gruyter, 1986, 368-89 (and the excellent bibliography).

3    J.H. Hayes, 'Israel', *Mercer Dictionary of the Bible*, Macon, GA: Mercer Press, 1989, 417-20.

sense of the biblical literature and yet so wide-ranging and so flexible. What is the significance of the ideological play evident in the term and in the different historical contexts in which it may be rooted or to which it may refer? It is no adequate treatment of the term merely to list the uses, explain the differences and stop there. It may be true that, for example, naming Jacob 'Israel' is a secondary definition, or that the term can acquire sectarian connotations, but these observations hardly recognize just how problematic is the question of defining 'Israel' on its biblical terms.

Quite apart from the theological bias inherent in the discipline, to which I referred at the end of the last chapter, there is an obvious reason for this oversight: over-exposure to the literature. Familiarity with the Bible from an early age, including membership of a Christian congregation, has the effect of conforming the imagination and the structures of one's thought to the Bible's own. Most biblical scholars have a long acquaintance with the Bible, and its notion of 'Israel' has already been internalized in their minds, to the point where they take its multifarious uses to be homogeneous, its complexity to be simple and its contradictory to be invisible. The notion of a biblical 'Israel' is so familiar, so ingrained, that a critical analysis of its usage never occurs as a necessity.[4] The 'Israel' of the biblical literature is automatically adopted as a term appropriate for scholarly use, including all its variety and contradiction. 'Israel' is a people; 'Israel' has a religion; 'Israel' has its own proper god; 'Israel' is really two kingdoms; 'Israel' is strictly one kingdom; 'Israel' is a land, etc. All this makes sense until or unless an unfamiliar critic takes the stage, or one who has taken steps to de-familiarize himself or herself (a step which is counter to the theological instinct!)

Before embarking on a critical definition of the *historical*, as opposed to the *biblical* Israel, then, it seems a good idea to dispose of the biblical Israel as a ready-made entity, or even as a starting point, for an historical investigation. For this purpose, what is required is not a fully-fledged account of the biblical Israel as an ideological concept, but something a little simpler: an analysis of the biblical criteria, implied or otherwise, by which this biblical Israel is

---

4    A partial exception is H.G.M. Williamson, 'The Concept of Israel in Transition', in R.E. Clements (ed.) *The World of Ancient Israel*, Cambridge, 1989, 141-159; but Williamson is thinking of a concept already established and being refashioned.

historically defined. In other words, what, in the view of the biblical literature itself, constitutes 'Israel'? How does the term function within the literature, and why does it function in this way?

### Critique of the biblical Israel

A scan of the various definitions of biblical 'Israel' offered earlier yields three categories of criteria: ethnic, religious and political. Some of the individual usages in fact cross these categories. Nos. 1-2 and 8-9 listed above are ethnic (ancestor, tribes); nos 3-5 are political (kingdoms), and no. 10 is religious. Of the others, no. 6, the 'community/*Gemeinde* is defined on both cultic (religious) and ethnic criteria, and no. 7 ('Israel' as opposed to 'Aaron') is, formally speaking, ethnic (the use of the ancestor name 'Aaron' determines this). I repeat that this classification is not hard and fast, and there is overlap. It matters only that three kinds of criteria, political, ethnic and religious, adequately cover the various uses. Indeed, both in the biblical and the scholarly literature, the term 'Israel' is generally used in more than one of these senses simultaneously. It is precisely because the three categories are not entirely compatible that the problem of definition, at least from the historian's point of view, arises.

We must keep in mind these three sets of criteria when considering the historical implications of the biblical usages. In any given historical context, which meaning yields sense, if any? But there is another dimension to the problem: at what are we looking in order to try and provide this biblical 'Israel' with an historical context? We are looking, of course, at the population of Palestine, especially in the Iron Age, though also in the Persian period, which the biblical literature also partly covers. But because of the variability of the biblical definition, we cannot automatically identify any such population as the biblical 'Israel'. We shall have apply the three criteria before we decide whether it is legitimate or accurate to describe these people as 'Israel' in the biblical sense. It is true that the inhabitants of Palestine can be regarded as the historical *counterpart* to biblical 'Israel', because both occupy the same time and space in human history, but one of the two is an archaeologically attested population about whom we know fairly little, while the other is the literary concept about whom we know everything (since everything that pertains to them falls inside the Bible!). Are we, using purely historical methods, entitled to superimpose one on the other? My point here is that we cannot (despite traditional practice) proceed to this identification until we first have an adequate working definition of the biblical 'Israel'—which we do not possess. We cannot automatically transfer any of the characteristics of the biblical 'Israel' onto the pages of Palestine's history. To put it again, another way (for the point is crucial): in seeking to establish whether and if so, how far, the biblical 'Israel' exists as a real historical population or society, we cannot take the conclusion as the premise. *Do* the inhabitants of Iron Age Palestine in fact meet the criteria of the biblical 'Israel'—or vice-versa? In answering this question, just as we shall draw our definition of the biblical 'Israel' from the biblical literature, so we shall have to draw our definition of the people of Palestine from their own relics—and that means excluding the biblical literature. Unless we do this, the conclusion is, of course, pre-determined!

Let us begin, then, with the biblical Israel. It begins with the ancestor Jacob, who is given the name 'Israel' (though it is not used of him very often).[5] Hence, the term 'children of Israel' (often used synonymously with 'Israel') is presumably to be understood in this rather literal sense, as descendants of the eponym. Accordingly, the 'children of Israel' consist of twelve 'tribes', each traced back to a son (or grandson) of Jacob/Israel. These 'tribes' originate in Palestine[6] (which is called, among other names, 'Canaan'), migrate to Egypt, where they are enslaved, then escape and after wandering between Egypt and their destination for forty years, conquer the 'land of Canaan', though not completely. Thereafter they are ruled by 'judges' who 'judge' 'all Israel' (though their exploits are always confined to one 'tribe' or, in one case, to a group of 'tribes'). They later elect a king, Saul; he is killed, and then succeeded by another, David, who is already king of Judah (which may or may not be one of the tribes ruled by Saul), but becomes king of a kingdom of the twelve 'tribes' called 'Israel', although within this kingdom the 'house of Israel' and the 'house of Judah' are distinguished. David rules over an empire from the borders of Egypt to the Euphrates, as does his successor, Solomon. Under Solomon's successor, the kingdom redivides into 'Judah' and 'Israel', the latter being regarded as religiously

5    Gen. 32.28; 35.10,21-22; 37.3,13, etc.
6    Since this is where the tribal; ancestors are born. However, it is only in Egypt that the sons are addressed as tribes by (Israel)/Jacob (Gen. 49.28).

illegitimate. Israel (i.e. the northern kingdom) falls to the Assyrians and later Judah falls to the Babylonians. Its rulers are deported, but after about fifty years are allowed to return to Judah. Some do so, and rebuild Jerusalem and its Temple, instituting the law of Moses and preserving their ethnic purity. Yet 'Israel' continues to include the descendants of the former kingdoms still living elsewhere, whose return is often hoped for.

It is commonly granted that this picture is to some extent idealized, with many historically impossible or unlikely elements. But it is not appreciated just how impossible it is for an historian to introduce such an 'Israel' into the history of Iron Age Palestine, even in a modified form. Let me focus on two issues which I hope will illustrate this impossibility. Although 'Israel' is generally used to denote that which split into the two kingdoms of Israel and Judah, the terms 'house of Judah' and 'house of Israel' suggest that the ethnic definition applies strictly to the kingdom of Israel; 'house' here can hardly mean 'dynasty', and persumably means 'descendants of the family of Israel (Jacob)' This interpretation coheres with the use of the name 'Jacob' when applied to the kingdom of Israel (i.e. the northern of the two which comprise the larger 'Israel'). We thus have a strong thread running through the biblical literature which accords the name 'Israel' primarily (even exclusively at times) to only one kingdom. On the other hand, 'all Israel' denotes Israel and Judah together. However, Second Isaiah often uses 'Jacob' when addressing Judaeans, and Judah is presented (sometimes) as the eldest son of Jacob. Which is the *historical* Israel? Most biblical historians opt for the larger definition, and thus adopt the term 'northern kingdom' for the kingdom more strictly known as Israel. As noted earlier (note 1), Miller and Hayes have taken the other option in entitling their book *A History of Ancient Israel and Judah*. Obviously, had they simply written a history of Israel using their own definition, it would have been different from other histories in that it would have ended in the eighth century BCE. The 'northern' kingdom of Israel, then, is obviously historical in a way that the twelve-tribe Israel is not, and as much can be deduced from reading the biblical literature itself.

A second issue is that of 'Canaanites'. The notion of a clear opposition between 'Canaanites' and 'Israelites' is fundamental to much of the biblical literature, and basic to most scholarly histories too. By means of this concept, 'Israel' can be distinguished as a stranger in the land it has entered, by virtue of its ethnic and cultural separation from the indigenous population. The distinctions are enforced respectively in the biblical literature by a ban on intermarriage and on religious imitation. (Thanks to the discoveries at Ras Shamra, scholars think they are even able to describe for us what 'Canaanite' religion really was.)

But outside the biblical literature the 'Canaanites' refuse the same neat definition. As already noted, there is no non-biblical evidence of an ethnic distinction: the people living where biblical Israel is located did not come from outside, and were not ethnically distinct, nor is there evidence of their having a different culture from other occupants of Palestine. In a recent study of the subject, N.-P. Lemche has demonstrated that even the name 'Canaan' cannot be shown from the non-biblical evidence to have a consistent usage. Sometimes it designated the coastland, sometimes all of Palestine, sometimes a more specific area.[7] There is no definitive 'land of Canaan', and 'Canaanites' cannot be used with any precision by an historian of Palestine. Now, once again we find that the biblical literature, tendentious though it is, is actually more careful than many historians who have depended upon it. For while it occasionally speaks of Canaanites (or 'Amorites'), it is also sometimes aware that these people contain many different ethnic groups (e.g. Hivites, Perizzites, Hivites, Girgashites). It is apparent that the population of Palestine in the Iron Age was not at all ethnically homogeneous; nor was it politically united. It is hard to state the criteria for a 'Canaanite'. The point is, surely, that for the biblical literature 'Canaanites' are simply indigenous non-Israelites.

So Israel cannot be distinguished from Canaan because Israel, as far as it histrically exists, is part of Canaan, culturally fairly homogeneous while ethnically mixed. The historian, then, cannot really work with this ethnic-cultural criterion of Israel. The criterion could be applied only if an Israelite state existed which contained only people of a single ethnic and cultural identity. If this condition does not apply, as it does not (not even on the biblical description), the distinction between 'Canaan' and 'Israel' becomes incoherent because the ethnic/cultural and the political contradict one another. For instance, if we take the simple example of Yhwh-worship, we have

---

7    N.-P. Lemche, *The Canaanites and their Land: The Tradition of the Canaanites* (JSOTS, 110), Sheffield: JSOT Presss, 1990.

this difficulty: in a kingdom called Israel, which consists of those worshipping Yhwh and those not worshipping Yhwh, and with no ethnic correspondence to the cultic affiliation, who are the Israelites? A subject of the king of Judah whose name is Uriah and is called a Hittite (one of the nations of Canaan, Gen. 15.20; Deut. 7.1; 20.17) is presumably a 'Canaanite'. Thus, it is not the case that Canaanites are necessarily not Yhwh-worshippers, nor that they lie outside of the political definition of 'Israel'. Do we know that, on the criteria offered by the Bible and followed by biblical scholarship, Bathsheba is supposed to be an 'Israelite' woman (or Judaean)? No sensible historian is going to get embroiled in this kind of distinction. If there are, ultimately, some sets of distinctions that can be made on the basis of maximal lineages or whatever, we are unable to exercise them in our present state of knowledge, and they certainly cannot be arrived at via the crudely ideological biblical distinctions. In any case, I am suggesting that for the historian's purpose they are hardly of much value.

And if there are no 'Canaanites', there can be no 'Israelites'. Or, put another way, if Canaanites are inhabitants of the 'land of Canaan' taken to mean Palestine, what sort of 'Canaanites' are the 'Israelites'? And would being 'Israelite' have anything to do with being ruled by a king of 'Israel'? The biblical concept requires, and perhaps even seeks to project, the notion of a nation-state in which being Israelite is both a political and religious definition. But the biblical literature itself also explodes that concept by stating that the 'Canaanites' were not expelled, and that 'Israel' adopted 'Canaanite' cultural practices.

In fact, the historian must in the end be driven back to the only workable definition, namely the political: a *political* entity in the strict sense, a kingdom occupying the northern Palestinian highlands, whose capital was (finally) Samaria. This political entity consisted of different population elements who worshipped deities under the names of Yahweh, Baal, El and Asherah (and probably more). Both biblical and non-biblical sources agree on this religious diversity, except that the biblical material operates with an ideal 'Israel' by means of which this historical 'Israel' is judged to have deserted its true religion and its true political allegiance, as well as being only a part of the 'ideal Israel', namely ten-twelfths of it. The ideal 'Israel' corresponds in the biblical literature to such an historical definition only in the kingdom of David and Solomon; but, as we shall see in the next chapter, this 'united kingdom' will probably have to be abandoned as minimally historical if historical at all. In any case–and this is what really matters–the historian is obliged to deal with the population that actually lived in this land, *their* way of life, *their* religion, laws, and institutions. No historian who attempts to do this will end up with a picture recognizable as the biblical 'Israel'. There will be an historical kingdom called Israel, but with none of the definitive characteristics of the biblical 'Israel', not even as a rebellious 'Israel' deserting the 'Davidic dynasty'. It will be ethnically and religiously mixed. The biblical literature, on the other hand, implies an Israel (political) within an 'Israel' (ethnic) as well as an 'Israel' (ethnic) within an Israel (political), the impossible result of a clash of incommensurate definitions.

Another case in which the biblical literature deconstructs, as it were, its own presentation is the 'exile', a problem to which I referred in the previous chapter in respect of the scholarly construct of the scholarly 'ancient Israel'. According to the biblical account, the 'exile' was a punishment upon the nation–primarily the ruling class–for its infidelity to its deity. However, the biblical literature also presents 'Israel' two or three generations later as the descendants of these 'exiles', having become those who alone preserved the religion, and who, on their 'return', proceed to isolate themselves from the 'people of the land'. Biblical historians, it was noted, fondly imagine the deportees hugging their copies of Deuteronomy or transcripts of the oracles of Jeremiah to their chests, and spending evenings in Tel Abib ruminating on their plight and preserving the faith, developing their literature into long histories and bodies of law and huge collections of oracles, all the while longing to return to 'Zion' (i.e. Jerusalem). It is hard for any historian to justify following the history of 'Israel' (even if, for the sake of the argument, it is taken to include Judah) through the deported population and then back into Yehud, rather than through the remaining population (which was no doubt augmented by immigrants from neighbouring territories, if not by other Babylonian deportations unmentioned by the Bible).[8] But the 'returnees' are described in the biblical literature as enforcing their claims to be the

---

8    It is well known that Martin Noth, in his *History of Israel*, London: A. & C. Black, 1958, acknowledged that those left in the land deserved to be considered by the historian of ancient Israel, but while he has been followed by a few others, the bulk of biblical scholarship continues to be obsessed with the fate of the 'exiles'.

true 'Israel' through observance of the law and ethnic purity, both criteria very hard to establish objectively. Orthodoxy (or orthopraxy) in Iron Age societies is not defined in this way. My point is that here, again, the biblical literature is defining an ideological Israel which is actually not hard to understand, though it cannot be confused with an historical one, which would virtually reverse the identification.

In describing the Persian periods the biblical literature confines its Israel to the province of Yehud, and here as clearly as anywhere it justifies that label by ethnic and religious-cultic criteria. Yet the inhabitants of the region of Samaria and later the Samaritans (whatever continuity if any there is between these groups) both have some claim to be included in the history of 'Israel', the former by their geographical location, the latter by their adoption of the 'law of Moses'. There is no reason for the historian to endorse the monopolistic claim to this title of the inhabitants of Yehud, as biblical historians almost invariably do. For at this point 'Israel' as a political entity exists in the past only, and claims to that past require to be judged impartially. It is only in the Hasmonean period (of which the biblical literature does not directly speak) that the term 'Israel' again acquires a political connotation, and, with forcible conversion of non-Judaeans, the issue of what defines an 'Israelite' recurs. Prior to that moment, the definition of Israel can only be an ideological one; although a case could be made for saying that it was a cultic one, that would not suffice to explain the choice of 'Israel' as a name.

There are other reasons that stand in the way of an historian transferring the biblical 'Israel' onto the historical stage, but these involve data external to the biblical literature. In this chapter I have wanted to show simply that it is impossible to pretend that the biblical literature provides a clear enough portrait of what its Israel is to justify an historical interpretation and application. The historian thus needs to investigate the real history independently of the biblical concept. The issue is not, as many scholars misunderstand it, one between biblical and non-biblical data, between 'archaeology and the Bible'. It rests simply in the fact that the biblical construct is evidently ideological and cannot even on its own terms be translated into an historical one; the criteria by which this could be done are simply either too slippery, or invalid or contradictory. That leaves historians with no choice but to choose their own term for the society or societies they are looking for in Iron Age highland Palestine. And they must be guided by what these societies have left themselves, for it is not yet clear that the biblical literature is any part of their bequest.

I have now dealt in successive chapters with the 'ancient Israel' of the scholars and with the Israel of the biblical literature. Neither is an historical construct. It is time to turn to that which is, including the historical Israel.

Chapter Four

## A SEARCH FOR HISTORICAL ISRAEL

Given the incommensurability of the biblical Israel with any historical people or state, there can be no question of taking those elements from the biblical literature that are historically plausible or even those that have historical counterparts, and grafting them onto the history of Iron Age Palestine. There is no way to judge the distance between the biblical Israel and its historical counterpart *unless the historical counterpart is investigated independently of the biblical literature.* To many biblical scholars, such a procedure seems unnecessarily anti-biblical, sceptical or negativistic. Unless the argument has been thought through, it can indeed seem pereverse to ignore so much information, so temptingly realistic and specific. But I hope it is now clear that unless this is done, there can be no basis for claiming that the biblical 'Israel' *has* any particular relationship to history. The biblical literature simple cannot be used to verify itself, and we have no choice in the matter if we are going to avoid arguing in the circle I described in chapter 1.

Our next task, then, is to discern, as far as our sources permit, within the history of the peoples of Palestine during the time and in the areas covered by the biblical Israel, the population and/or state to which the name 'Israel' *historically* belongs. Obviously, the artifacts these people left, the buildings they occupied, and the literature they certainly wrote (i.e. datable inscriptions) are the primary evidence. And by what criterion are we going to discern this historical Israel? In the first place, by the name.

### *The name 'Israel'*

Of the ultimate origin of the name 'Israel' we are really in the dark. According to a Ugaritic text (*KTU* 4.623.3), the name *ysr'l* was borne by a Maryannu warrior. Indeed, a name with a theophoric component suggests to many a person rather than a place.[1] But there is probably no connection between this particular individual and the Israel we are investigating. The same cannot be said with equal confidence about the so-called 'Merneptah Stele' or 'Israel Stela'.[2] Here is a reference to an 'Israel' dating from the end of the 13th century BCE. The relevant portion of text reads:

> The princes lie prostrate, saying 'shalom'
> None raises his head among the Nine Bows
> Tehenu destroyed, Hatti pacified
> Canaan is plundered with every misery
> Ashkelon is taken, Gezer is captured
> Yanoam has been made non-existent
> Israel lies desolate; its seed (*prt*) is no more
> Hurru has become a widow for To-meri [Egypt]
> All lands together have become peaceful
> Everyone who was a nomad has been reined in by king.....Merneptah

There seems no doubt that the location of Merneptah's Israel lies somewhere in Palestine; the dispute over this text concerns whether the name indicates a land or a people. Ashkelon, Gezer and Yanoam are marked with a determinative sign identifying them as city-states, whereas Israel is marked with one which signifies peoples either not living in cities, or transhumants. The determinative is not unambiguous and could, it seems, be used of an area in which there were no city-states. Much also depends on whether the word 'seed' denotes human offspring or crops (though the former is perhaps better supported).

It is possible that the Israel of this inscription is the name of a population living, presumably, in the highlands of Palestine. But the name given to this people may equally be derived from the name of the place. If not, however, might we not begin the history of Israel

---

1 So E.A. Knauf, review of G. Ahlström, *Who Were the Israelites?*, *JNES* 49 (1990), p. 82. But see O. Margalith, 'On the Origin and Antiquity of the Name Israel', *ZAW* 102 (1990), pp. 225-237. Names like 'Bethel' and 'Penuel' seem obvious counter-examples.

2 For recent discussion of the text see L. Stager, 'Merenptah, Israel and Sea Peoples: new Light on an Old Relief', *Eretz Israel* 18 (1985), pp. 56-64; D. Redford, 'The Ashkelon Relief at Karnak and the Israel Stele', *IEJ* 36 (1986), pp. 190-200; F.J. Yurco, 'Merenptah's Canaanite Campaign', *Journal of the American Research Center in Egypt* 23 (1986), pp. 189-215; G. Ahlström, 'The Origin of Israel in Palestine', *SJOT* 2 (1991), pp. 19-34 (27-34). Most recently, see the debate between Yurco and A.F. Rainey in *BAR* 17/6 (1991), pp. 56-61.

here? Many scholars believe so. The importance of the Merneptah
stele is to show that the name 'Israel' goes back at least to the 13th
century BCE. But does it also give us the starting point for the hisory
of a particular population or society? Before answering this question,
we had better reflect on the issues a little further. What is at issue in
the name?

A recent wail of protest from an influential journalist bemoaned the
disappearance of 'Israel' from the Late Bronze/Early Iron period [c.
1250–1050] as follows:[3]

> [People want to learn] what plausibly can be said about the
> premonarchical history of Israel. Not about the people of the central hill-
> country, mind you, but about the Israelites. The settlement of the central
> hill-country of Canaan in Iron Age I is of special interest because these
> settlements are thought to be Israelite. People want to know what
> happened here and what it meant to be Israelite. If these people were not
> Israelites, they have as much interest to us as Early Bronze Age IV
> people. That does not mean we are uninterested, but it does mean
> considerably less interest than if they were Israelites. In short, we want to
> know what all this evidence—and there is plenty of it—can plausibly tell us
> about early Israel....

Thus Hershel Shanks expresses the problem eloquently, though
perhaps not very sophisticatedly (though his more serious problem is
perhaps economic, namely how as an editor of a biblical archaeology
magazine he might manage without his star item!). So what *is* entailed
by the use or non-use of the term 'Israel' for the population referred
to by Merneptah? Is the issue whether these people also *called
themselves 'Israel'*? Or whether they are in the course of time to
become a state bearing the name 'Israel'? Or is it enough that they are
occupying the same space as the biblical 'Israel'? For Shanks, and for
many other laymen, and even some scholars, the name itelf is what
counts. But names and historical identities do not belong together in
the simple way that such arguments suppose. For instance, Scotland
takes its name from a people (the ancient Scots) who crossed the Irish
Sea and settled in Ireland; to the extent that the Scots are descended
from any ancient people, these are the Picts, while the Irish are the
descendants of the ancient Scots. The modern 'British' are not the
Britons of the Roman period, and mostly not descended from them,
for those Britons were driven into what is now Wales and parts of

3    Hershel Shanks, 'When 5,613 Scholars Get Together in One Place: The
Annual Meeting, 1990', *BAR* 17/2, March/April 1991, p. 66.

Cornwall by Angles and Saxons who originated in Germany (not to mention Danes and Normans). The Dutch are not the *Deutsch*. Nor, to go further afield, is the modern country of Ghana on the same territory as the 18th century West African state of Gana from which it is named. Modern Palestinians share a label with ancient Philistines, and modern Israelis with Israelites, but in neither case is there really a very strong connection. Many modern Palestinians might in theory be able to trace their ancestry back three thousand years to inhabitants of Palestine; but during their history these ancestors will have changed into Judaeans, Christians, and now (most of them) Muslims. On the other hand, many modern citizens of Israel do not have an ancestor who ever lived in the territory occupied by the historical Israel (which is actually the West Bank, not the coastal plain where Tel Aviv, Ashkelon, Netanya and Haifa are!). As will be observed later, populations change a lot in the ancient Near East and labels need to be used with due caution: the inhabitants of the land known to the Assyrians as *pilaštu* and to the Romans as Palestina were not 'the Philistines'.

In the case of this early Israel of the Merneptah stele such considerations are important. For the next attestation of an Israel in this region is in an inscription of Shalmaneser III (c. 853) which refers to Ahab of *šr-il-la-a-a* (with the denominative for land [*mat*]). (The inscription of Mesha, king of Moab, follows shortly after, c. 840). Between these references and Merneptah lie over 350 years, a period much longer than the lifetime of the United States of America! During that time, what kind of continuity can we assume, which might enable us to speak, in an historical way, of the 'Israel' whose definition we take from the biblical literature? In terms of population, very little, as we shall now see.

### The population from which Israel was composed

Thanks to fairly recent Israeli surveys in the present West Bank, we are now able to trace the remains of the settlers in the Palestinian highlands who perhaps correspond to Merneptah's Israel. Previous attempts to find archaeological traces had confined themselves to the ruins of Palestinian cities, pinning their hopes on finding evidence of a conquest by non-'Canaanite' groups. But the conquest theory is now abandoned and Alt's model of a gradual settlement in non-populated areas is being confirmed. At the present time, there is a remarkable consensus among those few scholars who have specialized on the problem of these early settlers.[4] I. Finkelstein, whose fieldwork has been crucial in establishing this consensus, sums up its lines as follows:[5]

> –There was no political entity named Israel before the late-11th century.
> –The people who formed this entity came from diverse backgrounds– groups of sedentarizing nomads, withdrawing urban elements, northern people, groups from the southern steppe, etc.
> –The settlement process was basically a peaceful one, with local skirmishes, especially in a later phase of the period.
> –The ethnic lines between the settling groups were vague and the ethnic affiliations merged together with the rise of the political powers. Most of the biblical material represents more the way that the Israelite origin was grasped in Jerusalem of the late monarchic period than an accurate account of the emergence of Israel.

This ethnically heterogeneous, culturally indigenous group of settlers were bound together by their particular lifestyle, and they lived in villages. Over a period of time, their highland villages, many established in clearings, developed into a more integrated population. This population became, in turn, a state. In reconstructing this process we have to rely on models derived from a widespread study of social and state formation. Such study has taught us two things of particular relevance in this case. First is that a society is created as a structure, and that kinship becomes an organizing principle of societies in the early phase of development, both in practice and in principle. In practice, both the retention of village and family property, and, as a corollary, the formation of political and economic alliances between families and between villages take place through marriage. In this way, geographical and economic relations come to function also in

4    Among the burgeoning volume of literature on the Iron Age population of the Palestinian highlands may be cited D. Hopkins, *The Highlands of Canaan: Agricultural Life in the Early Iron Age* (SWBA, 3), Sheffield: Almond Press, 1985; R.B. Coote and K.W. Whitelam, *The Emergence of Israel in Historical Perspective* (SWBA, 5), Sheffield: Almond Press, 1987; I. Finkelstein, *The Archaeology of the Israelite Settlement*, Jerusalem: IES, 1988; *SJOT* 2 (1991); G. Ahlström, *The History of Ancient Palestine*, Sheffield: JSOT Press, 1992; T.L. Thompson, 'From the Stone Age to Israel,' *Proceedings of the Midwest Regional Meeting of SBL, 1991*, (forthcoming).

5    I. Finkelstein, 'The Emergence of Israel in Canaan: Consensus, Mainstream and Dispute', *SJOT* 2 (1991), pp. 47-59, 56.

terms of kinship–we might say, ethnicity. On the other hand, kinship also operates as a code in which relationships of power are described and quantified. Thus, in such societies, genealogies function not as lists accurately transmitted through time, but as descriptions of political and economic relations, amenable to revision, and always a fluid mixture of genuine kinship links and fictitious ones. The second point is that the evolution of such societies towards a state, in which will emerge a ruling caste or a dominant family and then a chieftain, later to become a king, is a regular process, and no specific external causes need to be postulated for that process. The chief, or king has an army, and a capital. He raises taxes in some kind to support his hegemony. These are the essential ingredients and they develop in a fairly logical fashion. 'States happen', we might say.[6]

Accordingly, we can project the development of this society from its earliest stages until it emerges as a state. At this point it may be treated as a political as well as a social entity. Whether, or at what point, this evolving society is entitled to be called 'Israel' is a matter of judgment. We can say at the very least that a state which will be referred to by others as 'Israel' is being *formed* during this process, developing from a settlement of small clearing villages, then becoming a society of villages, and then in the course of time a kingdom. And this process of formation seems to me part of the history of the historical Israel, or perhaps more correctly, part of the pre-history of Israel.

So long as the state remains basically co-extensive with the society from which it grew, the ethnic and the political character do not conflict. In fact, it can be allowed that while the villages are in the process of combining into a more cohesive society, through various forms of agricultural and military cooperation and the practice of exogamy, a certain ethnic identity will in fact develop, both literally (to an extent) and socio-politically, since genealogy is a code for defining social relations. However, the boundaries of a society and the boundaries of a state do not necessarily coincide beyond the point where the state seeks to enlarge its boundaries beyond the society from which it emerged[7]. At this point the state and the society will not

6    For a very thorough treatment of this question, see F.S. Frick, *The Formation of the State in Ancient Israel : A Survey of Models and Theories* (SWBA, 4), Sheffield: Almond Press, 1986.

7    I am dealing here exclusively with states that evolve by the essentially internal process of increasing complexity of social organization. There exists also a class of

be necessarily coextensive. For example, the (literary) state ruled by David was not a society. But neither states not societies remain static. By means of contact with contiguous societies, chiefly by trade, though also by intermarriage, and often as a result of warfare, societies change their boundaries; by means of warfare and diplomacy, states change theirs. It is thus obvious what difficulties confront the historian writing about historical Israel. It can be defined as a society or as a state, but hardly both. It may be that the name 'Israel' originated as a name of a society. However, the history of a state is much more tangible. States, comprising kings, armies and large cities, are more easily identified from literary records, though archaeologists are increasingly more interested in the rest of the population, the other ninety percent. At any rate, a state may well comprise several ethnic affiliations and various cults. It is especially important to bear these observations in mind in view of the equation of ethnos=state=religion found in the biblical literature (forgiveable, since this is literature, not history) but often also in the writings of biblical scholars (unforgiveable). So historical Israel is probably best defined by the historian as a state, i.e. a kingdom–which is how others seem to have referred to it (when they used the term at all), as we shall see.

### The Israelite state

Is it possible to fix dates for the establishment and the fall of the kingdom of Israel, or map its extent during this time? The inscriptions of Ashurnasirpal (883-859) do not refer to it. The earliest evidence we have is from Shalmaneser III's 'Kurkh stele' where 'Ahab the Israelite' is mentioned, while on the 'Black Obelisk' Jehu 'son of Omri' is mentioned (and depicted). Mesha king of Moab (c. 840) gives not only a reference to Israel but to its king Omri. Omri's son is mentioned, too, but not named. Adad-nirari III's expedition to Palestine in 803 (recorded in the Nimrud slab inscription) mentions Hatti-land, Amurru-land, Tyre, Sidon, $^{mat}Hu\text{-}um\text{-}ri$ (land of Omri), Edom, Philistia (Palestine?), and Aram (not Judah). His 'Rimah Stele'

so-called secondary states that are created by external factors, though such external factors do not include cooperation for the purpose of confronting an enemy (this being a process in the formation of a primary state). An overlord may set up a king with subjects as a buffer state, for example, or an area within a state may secede. The point is that in these cases the entire process of social formation does not take place.

mentions Joash of Samaria. Tiglath-Pileser III (743-732) mentions 'Menahem of Samaria' together with a list of other north Palestinian and Syrian kingdoms.[8] Finally, Sargon II describes his conquest of the city of Samaria, and also of 'the whole house of Omri'. Indeed, apart from the one reference to Jehu by Shalmaneser III, the regular Assyrian name for Israel is 'House of Omri' or 'land of Omri'. The only capital city mentioned is Samaria.[9]

The kingdom became vassal to Assyria as a result of the invasion of Tiglath-Pileser II; shortly afterwards it became an Assyrian province. By the time that Samaria fell, its territory had already nearly vanished, and what there was of it was incorporated into the Assyrian provincial system. The political history of historical Israel was at an end at this point. Although Samaria was rebuilt, there was to be no more state called 'Israel' in the strict sense. The history of 'Israel' was to be perpetuated thereafter in literary form.

### Judah

What, then, of the kingdom of Judah to the south, which in biblical histories carries on as the surviving part of 'Israel'? Here the problem is simply one of a complete absence of extra-biblical references. The biblical 'empire' of David and Solomon has not the faintest echo in the archaeological record–as yet. But the non-biblical evidence is hardly neutral. Evidence of the process of settlement in the Judaean highlands (which was a separate process from settlement in the highlands further north) makes it extremely difficult to conceive of the formation of a state until Iron IIB (900-800 BCE), and the formation of an empire of any size looks out of the question. The elaborate administration ascribed to David in the biblical literature is impossible at that stage, even if we are thinking of an Israelite and not a Judaean-Israelite state. Moreover, the failure as yet to establish archaeologically the history

8    The reference to *az-ri-a-u* (? ANET *ia-u-ha-zi*) $^{mat}$*ia-u-da-a* is seen by a minority of scholars (see e.g. *ANET*) as a reference to Azariah of Judah; the majority, however, identify the state in question as *Y'di*, mentioned in the Zinjirli inscription and located in northern Syria.

9    I might pose the question whether, in the absence of the biblical literature, historians would refer to this Palestinian kingdom as 'Israel' at all, rather than 'Omri-land' (and we would wonder who Omri was!); even in the biblical literature, the names 'Ephraim' and 'Samaria' are frequent alternatives. 'Israel' is a name which predominates only as a result of a later preference, and may not have been the name by which the state was most commonly known during its existence.

of Jerusalem in the Iron Age ought to be regarded as troublesome. It is also true that the attribution of extensive building activity to Solomon at Gezer, Megiddo and Hazor depends upon the biblical data and is not a purely archaeological deduction. The one contemporary inscription that might have shed light on the emergence of Judah is the Great Karnak Relief commemorating the campaign of Sheshonq I (who appears in the Bible as Shishak, 1 Kings 14), which is accompanied by a list of the places plundered. Unfortunately, many of these are not identifiable with certainty, and the list is not in any discernible geographical order (In addition to this list, Sheshonq left a stele at Megiddo confirming his conquest of the city.[10]) It is recognized that Sheshonq's campaign was concentrated in territory either in or bordering on Israel (though Israel is not mentioned), while the territory apparently occupied by Judah is largely bypassed, although Edom seems to be mentioned.[11] The date of this campaign, according to the Karnak inscription, is the 21st year of the pharaoh, and unfortunately our knowledge of Egyptian chronology is insufficient to offer a precise date. (Not surprisingly, the biblical chronology places this event subsequent to the time of Solomon.)[12]

We are thus unable at present to reconstruct the limits of the Israelite kingdom. More significantly, we are unable to include in our reconstruction any kingdom uniting the territory of Israel and that of Judah. This kingdom, which exists at present exclusively in the biblical literature and the biblical scholarship dependent on it, remains

10    The stela was found in stratum IVB/5A at Megiddo. It is reproduced in A. Jepsen and K.-D. Schunck, *Von Sinuhe bis Nabukadnezar*, Berlin: Evangelische Verlagstanstalt, 1988, 4th edition, p. 147. See also G.I. Davies, *Megiddo* (Cities of the Biblical World), Cambridge: Lutterworth Press, 1986, p. 96.

11    For a discussion of the text, see J.H. Breasted, *Ancient Records of Egypt* IV, Chicago: University of Chicago Press, 1906-7; reprinted New York: Russell and Russell, 1962, vol IV, §709-22 (pp. 348-57). Cities mentioned include Megiddo, Taanach, Shunem, Bethshan, Rehob, Mahanaim, following the Jezreel valley and crossing the Jordan. Gibeon, Bethhoron and Aijalon are mentioned, but not Jerusalem. An attempt has been made by B. Mazar, 'The Campaign of Pharaoh Shishak to Palestine', SVT 4 (1957), pp. 57-66. Cf also S. Herrmann, 'Operationen Pharao Schoschenks I. am östlichen Ephraim,' *ZDPV* 80 (1964), pp. 55-79.

12    The historicity of the Davidic-Solomonic 'united kingdom' has been in recent years most fiercely attacked by Garbini, *History and Ideology*, pp. 21-32 and D.B. Redford, *Egypt, Canaan, and Israel in Ancient Times*, Princeton: Princeton University Press, 1992, a book which unfortunately appeared after the present volume had been virtually completed.

theoretical. Certainly, it seems unlikely that there was any original connection between the settlers of Judah and those of Israel, and Israel seems to have been more advanced than Judah in terms of settlement and thus political development. The idea of Israel breaking away from Judah is highly implausible. It is quite likely that Judah was formed as a secondary state perhaps in the 9th century, and possibly by the Assyrians. The reasons may have been both political (a troublesome neighbour to Samaria and Damascus) and economic (to exploit the olive oil industry with Jerusalem as the regional market for the southern highlands and Ekron, where recent excavations have found evidence of large-scale olive-oil production, as the industrial centre). But so far these proposals have to be tentative. The fact is that we know virtually nothing of the origins of Jerusalem from archaeological data. The evidence recently accumulated by Jamieson-Drake[13] at least shows the impossibility of a Davidic empire administered from Jerusalem, and suggests that Judah became a state, and Jerusalem a major administrative centre, only in the 8th century BCE *at the earliest.* Earlier studies on the formation of the Judaean state, as Jamieson-Drake points out, describe the possible emergence of chiefdoms, which is still a far cry from the emergence of a monarchic state. The range of indices considered by Jamieson-Drake make it necessary for us to exclude the Davidic and and Solomonic monarchies, let alone their 'empire' from a non-biblical history of Palestine. Assyrian and Babylonian records, at any rate, do not refer to Judah until just before the fall of Samaria (c. 734 BCE).[14]

It is a clear implication from the probable dating of the Judaean monarchy that it is unlikely to have evolved independently of the relatively powerful state of Israel. Thus, although we have no extra-biblical evidence that Judah was ever thought of as Israel, it is possible to conceive that the two kingdoms were, in the eyes of the kingdom of Israel and perhaps even in Judah, part of 'greater Israel'. This state of affairs would offer one historical basis for the subsequent adoption of the identity of 'Israel' by inhabitants of the Jerusalem state, if that is

13  *Scribes and School in Monarchic Judah: A Socio-Archeological Approach* (SWBA, 9), Sheffield: Almond Press, 1991; see especially pp. 48-80 and the charts, pp. 199-204 on settlement and land use and pp. 81-106 and charts, pp. 205-7 on public works. For a rebuttal of alternative points of view and a synthesis, see pp. 136-159.

14  Tiglath-Pileser III refers to a *Ia-u-a-zi* of *Ia-u-da-a-a*, i.e. Yehoahaz (=Ahaz) of Judah (so Miller-Hayes, *History*, p. 341; *ANET*, p. 282).

what happened. Another possibility is that after the fall of Samaria, and/or in the Assyrian ravages which preceded it there was a sizeable migration of population to the still nominally independent erstwhile Israelite satellite to the south. There is evidence, though inconclusive, that Jerusalem, and the Judaean kingdom, increased in size during the period following the end of Israel, perhaps as an outcome of such migration–though the later reduction in Judaean territory after Hezekiah's capitulation might account for this also. At any rate, it is not unlikely that Judah contained a significant Israelite population in the 7th century. Certainly, with the later decline of Assyrian power, the territory of the Assyrian provinces in northern Palestine and Syria would have been coveted by a number of its neighbours–Egypt, Damascus and quite probably Judah too. Thus there are several possible contexts for the absorption of remnants of Israel into Judah, whether or not any of Judah's population actually regarded Judah as being part–the surviving part!–of Israel. But there are other equally or more plausible contexts too for the adoption of the name 'Israel' by Judaeans, and the rise of the biblical notion of a twelve-tribe Israel with Judah as the senior partner certainly has to be set later; there is no discernible reason for this development in the monarchic period. The narratives of the conquest, in both Joshua and Judges, the narratives of Saul and David and the account of the histories of the two kingdoms, all of which reverse the probable historical state of affairs and make Judah (in this case including Benjamin) into the first conqueror of the land, the provider of the first divinely-favoured king and founder of the only authentic dynasty, home of the national shrine, serve no evident purpose at this point in the history of the kingdoms of Palestine. Who would need persuading of what by such fictions?

### The religion of Israel and Judah

In discussing this topic, many biblical scholars assume that the singular 'religion' is to be taken literally. But no doubt several cults existed in each kingdom: city cults, dynastic cults, and popular cults. Relying again purely on the non-biblical evidence (which in this case is not really contradicted by the biblical story) we can partly describe the religious profile of Israel. In his inscription Mesha describes dragging the 'vessels of Yhwh' from Nebo (a sanctuary on Mt Nebo?)

before his god Chemosh; this testifies to Yhwh being an Israelite deity, worshipped in a Transjordanian sanctuary in disputed territory. Inscriptions from Kuntillet 'Ajrud[15] likewise, refer to 'Yhwh of Samaria and his Asherah' and 'Yhwh of Teman and his Asherah'. That this is hardly a peripheral phenomenon seems confirmed by the Khirbet el-Qom inscription.[16] The countless female figurines which constitute the most common archaeological artifact in Palestine during this period attest devotion to other deities (even if, as some protest, they are not all to be conveniently dubbed as 'fertility figurines'; but they are hardly all children's dolls, either!). The Elephantine papyri, dating from the Persian period but written by a colony established in the monarchic period, mention 'Yahu' together with Bethel and Anath. The names of some of the Israelite kings are Yahwistic, and other Yahwistic names are attested.[17] Equally, however, we find non-Yahwistic names of both kings and others.[18] There were several sanctuaries in Israel, too, at Dan, Hazor, Bethshean, and elsewhere. As for Judah, we find mostly Yahwistic royal and non-royal names attested archaeologically.[19] However, the data are rather meagre. The temples discovered at Lachish, Beersheba, Ta'anek, Deir 'Alla and other places also show the proliferation of cult centres; perhaps these were all Yhwh shrines, but we ought not to assume that.

If we can say with some confidence that Yhwh was a major deity of the kingdom of Israel and Judah, we must be careful of making an equation between the cult of Yhwh and the territory or populations of

15   Datable to c. 800 BCE. For the text and concordance of all ancient Hebrew inscriptions, see now G.I. Davies, *Ancient Hebrew Inscriptions*, Cambridge: CUP, 1991 (pp. 78-82 for Kuntillet 'Ajrud).

16   Datable to c. 700 BCE. See Davies, *Ancient Hebrew Inscriptions*, pp. 105-6 and J.M. Hadley, 'The Khirbet el-Qom Inscription', *VT* 37 (1987), pp. 50-62; M. O'Connor, 'The Poetic Inscription from Khirbet el-Qom', *VT* 37 (1987), pp. 224-30.

17   E.g. the names Shemaryahu, Gaddiyahu, Yehau-eel in the Samarian Ostraca (*ANET*, p. 321).

18   From the Samarian Ostraca, for example, Elisha', Ba'lah, Meriba'al.

19   This is also true for Judaean names in the biblical literature - though we need to be aware that non-Yahwistic names can often be easily amended to Yahwistic ones. Thus, in the Lachish ostraca we find mostly Yahwistic names: Hoshaiah, Koniah, Hodaviah, Tobiah, Semachiah, Shemaiah etc., though Shallum and Jaddua are non-Yahwistic (*ANET*, pp. 321-2). For a survey of the data, see J. Fowler, *Theophoric Personal Names in Ancient Hebrew* (JSOTS, 49), Sheffield: JSOT Press, 1988.

these two kingdoms. There are other places in Syria and Cisjordan where Yhwh is attested as a deity; Tiglath-Pileser's annals refer to *az-ri-a-u* of *ia-u-da-a*, probably, rather than Azariah of Judah, the ruler of a kingdom Y'di, attested also in the Zinjirli inscription,[20] while king of Hamath named Iaubidi is mentioned in the annals of Sargon.[21] Letters from Arad, dating to the end of the seventh or beginning of the sixth century contain overwhelmingly Yahwistic names. Although it is usually assumed that Arad (whose destruction is presumably to be associated with the campaigns of the Babylonians[22]) lay within the territory of Judah at this time, one of the letters discovered there reads 'The king of Judah should know...' which suggests that the Judaean king is not the king of Arad. It seems reasonable to conclude, then, that Yh/Yhw/Yhwh was a well-known deity also outside Israel and Judah. That Yahwistic names are given to all the Judaean kings (after the perhaps unhistorical David, Solomon and Rehoboam period) may actually reflect the dependent status of the Jerusalem king upon the Samarian, and a consequent obligation to adopt the same royal patron deity. Possibly Yh/w/h was the deity of Jerusalem, though in this case it is strange that the city was not (re-)named after him but after another deity, Shalem. Yet, since Samaria was not named after Yhwh either, although the Kuntillet 'Ajrud inscription associates him with the city, the adoption of this deity may have been later than the naming of the city. Omri, after all, is not a Yahwistic name, nor Ahab. Jehu is the first Israelite king with a Yahwistic name, if indeed it *is* Yahwistic![23]

### Historical and literary Israels

From the above survey of non-biblical data, we can say that the name 'Israel' existed in Palestine from at least the beginning of the Iron

20  See D. Wiseman in D. Winton Thomas (ed.), *Documents from Old Testament Times*, Edinburgh: Nelson, 1958, pp. 54, 56.

21  *ANET*, p. 285. I cannot comment knowledgeably on Garbini's conclusion (*History and Ideology*, pp. 57-8) that *yah* is, like *el*, not only a name of a deity but also a generic term meaning 'god'. Several other instances of the name *yah* cited by Garbini seem to be valid, though not necessarily all.

22  See Miller-Hayes, *History*, pp. 417-19.

23  On Yahwism in Israel and Judah see Mark Smith, *The Early History of God*, San Francisco: Harper and Row, 1987; although it makes a number of traditional assumptions, the main thesis of the book seems to me approximately in the right direction, and the discussion fairly judicious.

Age, though whether it belonged to any particular population group or to some area remains disputed. But this is the source from which the historical society of the northern Palestinian highlands took its name, at least during the monarchy. This political entity lasted until 722 BCE, and did not have any distinctive ethnic identity, nor any religious unity. It is true, of course, that ethnicity is to a large extent a social and political development, and not a racial one. However, the creation of an ethnic Israel presupposes a recognised unit called 'Israel' in the first place, which can then be construed ethnically in the way that ancient societies did. The problem is that in a monarchic state there is no particular reason for this kind of process, since this new power structure creates to a very large extent the sort of social identity which ethnicising does. As for religious unity, the only sort of unity that a monarchic state could be said to have religiously would be a royal cult adopted officially as the national cult. It is not readily conceivable that a single cult could embrace the court, city and the peasant. Nor is there much need for religious unification beyond the ruling classes. Ninety-five percent of the population of Israel and Judah, if they worshipped Yhwh, surely used the name for a Baal-type deity. The 'religion of Israel' so beloved of biblical scholars is not an historical datum but a function of the biblical construct.

Thus, of the four criteria of the biblical 'Israel' which were noted in the previous chapter, two have been found to correspond to the historical Israel: the name 'Israel' and the political state, the kingdom. But the remaining two, the ethnic and religious are so far absent. This means that the biblical 'Israel' might conceivably have drawn upon an historical Israel to some degree. Yet the biblical Israel cannot be attributed to that historical Israel, of whose society, culture, and religion what we can discover does not afford any plausible explanation of why such a literary creation should arise. I suggested in an earlier chapter that biblical scholarship had assumed the sources of the biblical portrait to come from the portrait itself, as it were: Iron Age historical Israel produced the biblical Israel. The argument, I pointed out, was circular, since only by assuming the biblical Israel to be historical could one then posit such a creator. The question now is: could what we know of Iron Age Palestine have produced the idea of 'Israel'? Can we find in the non-biblical data any clues to the creation of 'Canaanites', to the monotheistic ideal, to an ethnic exclusivism, to a cult obsessed with purity? Where lay the conditions for these ideas to emerge? For what precise reasons, from which persons or groups, in what interests, do they arise? No obvious answers offer themselves. The 'Israel' of the biblical literature is a concept that has *no discernible setting during this time*. With a monarchic state ethnic identity is redundant if not counter-productive (and in this case certainly not based on any genuine ethnic distinction between 'Israel' and others), while religious homogeneity is neither attested, nor would it make a lot of sense. And whence the idea of invasion or settlement from outside the land? Whence the hatred of 'Canaanites'– and in any case, who are these 'Canaanites'? If we are to take seriously the nature of the biblical 'Israel' we must investigate seriously under what circumstances and for what reasons this kind of construct might have emerged. The Iron Age does not seem to provide either. And so we must move on. The search cannot confine itself to the historical Israel, nor to the period into which the biblical Israel is projected. If it has emerged that this biblical Israel is an idea, a concept, a construct, and not an historical society, then we have in a sense only redefined the object of our search. It remains to seek out the locus of that concept. Where did 'Israel' come from?

Chapter Five

THE SOCIAL CONTEXT OF THE BIBLICAL ISRAEL

From the point at which the Israel of history ceases, the problem and the historical method of our search for 'Israel' also change. From this point there is no Israel automatically definable as a political or social entity whose history can be charted. We have instead an ideal 'Israel', namely the entity created in the biblical literature, which, as we have seen, does not correspond to the real historical Israel. Moreover, it is not an ideal created from within that historical Israel either. The historical Israel does not offer the necessary conditions for the creation of the Israel which appears in the biblical literature. Whether or not nuggets of historical fact are to be found (and no doubt there are quite a few), their retrieval will do nothing to alter the basic distinction that has to be drawn between the historical Israel and the 'Israel' of the biblical literature, nor does it permit us to insist that within the historical Israel we shall find the basis for the biblical one.

The historical context for this biblical Israel lies elsewhere, but outside historical Israel and at a later time. Thanks to the Dead Sea Scrolls, we have *termini ad quem* for the existence of the bulk of this literature, and these range from the end of the third century BCE to the end of the first century CE. If, then, as the arguments of the preceding chapters urge, we cannot attribute this literature to the Iron Age population, it is tduring the Persian and Hellenistic periods that the biblical literature ought to have been composed, and it is within a society in this period that we shall now search for the preconditions which permitted and motivated the generation of that ideological construct which is the biblical Israel.

Our archaeological sources for Palestine in this period, alas, are even more meagre than for the Iron Age. Thus, while it is possible–as shown in the previous chapter–to write a sketch of the history of the inhabitants of Palestine, including the kingdom of Israel, without recourse to the biblical literature, it is more difficult relying on archaeological evidence to write even an outline of the society which produced the biblical literature and thus the biblical Israel. The task accomplished in the previous chapters, of creating a non-biblical profile and comparing it with the biblical one, cannot be done for the Persian and early Hellenistic periods. Indeed, it is here more than anywhere that even some of the most sceptical biblical historians have relied upon the biblical narrative for their data, reading the accounts of Ezra and Nehemiah as pretty much an accurate description of conditions and events at that time. So a rather delicate approach becomes necessary now. We shall need to keep one eye on the society or societies which may have wished to claim the name 'Israel' for themselves, and the other eye on the character of the biblical Israel itself. We can look for elements of convergence between the two, and, without being drawn into circular reasoning, suggest that the two bodies of data are at the very least consistent and in some cases offer positive correlation. In this chapter, then, it is the profile of the literary Israel which provides the focus, and the historical context, which we can in most cases sketch only very provisionally, will need to be specified with the aid of inference. One can hope that in the future the availability of more and more non-biblical data will confirm, modify or refute the inferences that are to be drawn. It is often protested that since we know so little of the Persian-early Hellenistic period, we cannot confidently commit ourselves to assigning the biblical literature to that time. This is nonsense, and has not prevented the 'exilic period' from being overloaded with literary works. However tentatively, we must try and do justice to the lines of argument which point to the fifth-third centuries BCE as the period during which nearly all of the biblical literature came into existence (Daniel and perhaps Esther, of course, are later).

### *Where does the name 'Israel' persist?*

Although the history of Israel as a political entity ends in 722 BCE, the name Israel will probably have persisted, and of course memories and records of the historical kingdom. The name 'Israel' is perpetuated most obviously in the biblical and related writings, but it will in the first instance have continued to be used by the populations of the region who earlier comprised the historical Israel. It is at any rate in the history of these populations that we have to look in the first instance for the emergence of the biblical Israel  Several populations, however, are involved in this search. First, we have those remaining in Samaria and its surrounding territories, the literal remnant of historical Israel. The population transfers undertaken by the Assyrians in the final years of the kingdom of Israel did not necessarily displace most of the population. Second are those who were forcibly immigrated into the territory of erstwhile Israel, who will have brought their own religions with them, but who may be expected, in the manner of ancient Near Eastern people, to have added the local deity (or deities) to their pantheon, or regarded him as the supreme local deity, or merged deities, and indeed perhaps to have adopted the name 'Israel'. The city of Samaria was after all rebuilt by the Assyrians and the cult of Yhwh will likely have continued in that city. There is evidence for this from a slightly later period[1] and the best explanation of this evidence is that the cult of Yhwh never departed from this region. The name 'Israel' may have persisted especially in that cult, with the deity Yah/Yahu/Yhwh worshipped as the 'god of Israel', most likely with a consort as previously. The population of Judah, among whom the cult of Yhwh was also prominent, suffered deportation too, both under the Assyrians and under the Babylonians. Accordingly we have to add as the third element in our list the population remaining in Judah after each deportation. Although there is no literary evidence, there may also have been an import of population into Judah by either Assyrians or Babylonians, a fourth candidate. Then, fifth and sixth, we have the Israelite and Judaean deportees and refugees, in Assyria, Syria, Babylonia and Egypt, who may also have had an interest in the name 'Israel'. The widespread cult of Yhwh we find in the Persian and Hellenistic periods is hard to explain if we do not take these populations into account.[2]

---

1   The Elephantine papyri (c. 410 BCE) give as Delaiah and Shelemaiah the names of Sanballat's sons, while the Wadi Daliyeh papyri list Yeshaiah and Hananiah as the sons of another Sanballat .(For the texts see respectively A.E. Cowley, *Aramaic Papyri of the Fifth Century B.C.*, Oxford: Clarendon Press, 1923 and more recently B. Porten in collaboration with J.C. Greenfield, *Jews of Elephantine and Aramaeans of Syene (Fifth Century BCE): Fifty Aramaic Texts with Hebrew and English Translations*, Jerusalem, 1974; F.M. Cross, 'Aspects of Samaritan and Jewish History in Late Persian and Hellenistic Times', *HTR* 59 (1966), pp. 201-11.

2   Cf. Morton Smith, *Palestinian Parties*, pp. 62-74.

But while allowing for the possible persistence of the name 'Israel' (or, as I think even more likely, 'god of Israel') among these groups, we have to acknowledge that the literary Israel of the Bible is not directly a product of these groups. They may indeed have a contribution to make in various ways, but insofar as we can guess about their social structure and ideology, it does not seem that either in Samaria or in Mesopotamia will we find either the physical, moral or ideological conditions for the biblical Israel. However, any such populations who adhered to the cult of Yhwh, or thought (or were made to think) that they had some ancestral connection with Palestine, might come to embrace as their own history and culture that magnificent creation of the writers of the biblical literature. It seems to me that in this way we can account finally for the wide spread of 'Jewish' communities through the Mediterranean area and beyond. However, the fact that these are called 'Jews'. i.e. Judaeans, even though not Judaean by birth or perhaps even recent ancestry, points us to the fact that the home of 'Israel' and of the cult of its god was known to be in Judaea. And, given the centrality of Judah in the biblical literature there can hardly be any doubt that this is where we need to look for the origin of the literary 'Israel'. That may be one of the few uncontroversial conclusions of this book! However, what is not widely recognized is that the Judaean society responsible for this literature is not only later than Iron Age Judah, but in fundamental ways very different from it. It is this marked difference, this fairly radical discontinuity, which enable us to place the formation of the literary Israel in one epoch and not the other.

### Post-monarchic Judah

How far the *population* of post-monarchic Judah was continuous with that of monarchic Judah is hard to say. The native king and his family had been removed to Babylon, and a wider deportation had taken place, though whether it was a deportation of the ruling classes and their retainers or also of some peasants is impossible to say. The ravages of military invasion in any case disrupt the population through widespread death and flight. The reduction of the population may have been as much as fifty per cent immediately.[3] The damage

3   The numbers or ratios of those deported, refugees, casualties and those left in Judah all seem impossible to estimate with any precision. See the calculations by

done to the city and its temple is also impossible to estimate. Unfortunately, we have no Babylonian account of the second campaign of 586 and the deportation which resulted. Either another king was appointed or the kingdom became a province ruled by a governor.[4] We know, again, little or nothing of the circumstances of the population in Judah, and only a little more about the deportees. We have a rations list from Babylonia which includes the name of the deported king, and a later bank archive purportedly naming Jewish clients among others.[5]

Deportation was a long-established custom, made an instrument of imperial control by Assyrians (though not at all monopolized by them), and used, as well as to punish, deter and pacify, also to import much-needed labour into the Mesopotamian heartland. It was customary for temple furniture, including images of the gods, to be removed. Official archives of the Judaean monarchy will have been either confiscated to Babylon, or, more probably, left in Judah, which still had to be administered. What is fairly certain is that the Judaean deportees will have had no further access to these administrative

W.F. Albright, *The Biblical Period from Abraham to Ezra*, New York: Harper and Row, 1965, pp. 84-87; S. Mowinckel, *Studien zu dem Buche Esra-Nehemia,* Oslo: Universitetsforlaget, 1964, I, pp. 93-98; J. Weinberg, 'Demographische Notizen zur Geschichte der nachexilischen Gemeinde in Juda', *Klio* 59 (1972), pp. 45-59. On Neo-Assyrian deportations, see B. Oded, *Mass Deportations and Deportees in the Neo-Assyrian Empire*, Wiesbaden: Harrassowitz, 1979.

4    The biblical account proposes a governor Gedaliah, whose name suggests a Yahweh-worshipper, thus probably a Judaean. This seems a little odd; either a native king (thus with royal authority) or a Babylonian governor would have seemed more plausible. A seal from Lachish reads *lgdlyhw 'sr 'l hbyt*, possibly belonging to this man, and suggesting that he held some office previously. A seal reading *ly'zyhw 'bd hmlk* is suggested by Miller-Hayes, p. 422 (on the basis of 2 Kings 25.23), as having belonged to an official of Gedaliah. It is therefore possible that Gedaliah was actually installed by the Babylonians as a king after all. In this case, the biblical literature is concealing that fact, maybe because its authors did not regard him as 'Davidic'? However, we can only speculate: a local member of the nobility with proven pro-Babylonian sympathies might after all have been selected as a governor.

5    For a discussion of what is known or guessed about Judaeans (or at least Yahweh-worshippers) in Babylonia, see conveniently E.J. Bickerman in W.D. Davies and L. Finkelstein (eds), *The Cambridge History of Judaism I: Introduction; The Persian Period*, Cambridge: CUP, 1984, pp. 142-58.

documents, and it is not easy to imagine that they were allowed to take with them any other scrolls (assuming such literature existed), since the point of deportation is to alienate people from their homeland. Of the life of the deportees, refugees or those remaining in Judah we actually know virtually nothing. The biblical literature's sparse data on life in Babylonia (mostly in Ezekiel) are of dubious reliability: it is biblical scholarship which has painted a fanciful portrait of religious fervour and furious literary creativity among Judaeans in Babylonia. There is little biblical evidence for any such activity and it goes against everything that we know or can infer about deported populations.

We can in fact add very little to the meagre data we have concerning Judaeans between Nebuchadrezzar and Cyrus. But, quite apart from the biblical accounts (which are certainly not to be taken as *prima facie* reliable),[6] we can reconstruct in broad outline the events likely to have taken place in what becomes under the Persian administration the province of Yehud, part of the satrapy of 'Beyond the River', which originally included also Babylon with the territory between the Euphrates and Egypt. (Perhaps significantly, this is the one historical period in which the land promised to Abraham in Genesis 15.18 exists as a political unit.) Our first recourse for the history of Yehud in the period is to Persian imperial policy. The most oft-quoted feature of this policy is the repatriation of previously deported groups, as declared in the 'Cyrus cylinder'.[7] Judaeans are not mentioned in this inscription, but the results of surveys carried out in the 1967-8 survey and published by Kochavi[8] reveal that while the

6    It is agreed that the history of the composition of Ezra–Nehemiah removes the biblical form of the literature some way from the events related. The historicity of Ezra is at the very least an open question, and the so-called 'memoir of Nehemiah', even if it is the work of Nehemiah, is not for that reason unimpeachable. Autobiography is a notoriously distorted form of history, as demonstrated in this very case by D.J.A. Clines, *What Does Eve Do To Help? and Other Readerly Questions to the Old Testament* (JSOTS, 94), Sheffield: JSOT Press, 1990, pp. 124-64; 'The Nehemiah Memoir: The Perils of Autobiography'.

7    For the text, see *ANET*, pp. 315-16.

8    M. Kochavi (ed.), *Judaea, Samaria and the Golan: Archaeological Survey 1967-1968*, Jerusalem: The Survey of Israel, 1972 [Hebrew]. For discussion of the results of this survey pertinent to the Achaemenid period, see K. Hoglund, 'The Achaemenid Context' in *Second Temple Studies*, pp. 54-72. My own discussion is

surrounding territories of the northern highlands and the Arabah
show a drop in the number of occupied settlements between Iron II
(the monarchic period) and the Persian period (defined as
immediately following it, i.e. post-587 in Judah), Judah itself shows a
25% increase. Nearly all of the additional settlements are small
unwalled villages. But these are mostly not once-inhabited sites now
resettled. Two thirds of the new sites had been uninhabited during
Iron II. A quarter of them are entirely new sites, on previously
uninhabited territory. It is hard not to associate these sites with a
repopulation of Yehud under Cyrus and/or his successors, especially
since the pottery evidence from these sites points to the end of the
sixth century for their occupation–i.e. indicating a short and thus
deliberate process.

These results do not suggest returning deportees drifting back to
their original home towns, but, as Hoglund argues, rather an
Achaemenid policy of deliberate ruralization. As Hoglund understands
the situation, such a policy implies that the Persians claimed the land
of Judah as imperial domain; this in turn means there would be no
land claims by either immigrants nor the indigenous population, and
thus no struggle, such as is often surmised, between returners and
remainers over land holdings. If the evidence is to be interpreted in
this way, it would seem that the notion of benevolent return to former
homelands under the Achaemenids is rather misleading; there seems
an element of coercion in the the process. The transportation of
populations within the empire for the purposes of economic
development (agriculture or building) was, in line with its
predecessors, also employed by the Persians.[9] Hence, the 'returnees' to
Yehud were not necessarily Judaean 'exiles' coming home,
beneficiaries of an enlightened policy of repatriation of wronged
exiles, but subjects of transportation, moved to under-developed or
sensitive regions for reasons of imperial economic and political
policy. Perhaps the ancestors of these new immigrants did come from
Judaea, as the biblical literature insists, but that should not be
assumed. Perhaps they came from all parts of Palestine, or perhaps
even from elsewhere. The claim made by the biblical literature that
these people are returning exiles is powerfully made, and is all but

based on Hoglund's.

9    See A. Kuhrt, 'The Cyrus Cylinder and Persian Imperial Policy', *JSOT* 25
(1983), pp. 83-97.

universally accepted. Yet it is not pig-headed scepticism that hesitates, but rather reflection and common sense. For whether originally from Judah or not, these people or their descendants would be likely to believe, or to claim that they were, indigenous. Indeed, the Persians may well have tried, in order to facilitate compliance with the process, to persuade these transportees that they were being resettled in their 'homeland', and examples of this ploy in the imperial history of humankind could be cited. In fact, as I shall remark presently, certain biblical stories (e.g. the Abraham stories, the Joshua conquest stories) may indicate a little doubt among some inhabitants of Yehud that they did inhabit the land as erstwhile natives. In short, the biblical claim of repatriation cannot be accepted as evidence by any historian without some reserve, and pending some confirmation from non-biblical sources we are better to adopt a neutral stance on the matter.

At all events, as Briant has sought to establish,[10] the Achaemenids advanced over their predecessors in creating collectives, often village groupings which were treated as corporate units for taxation purposes. Moreover, Hoglund cites evidence that 'the empire sought to maintain the administrative identity of such collectives by insuring their ethnic distinction from the surrounding populations by relegating them to specific enclaves'.[11]

It is striking that the situation created by such communities is not dissimilar to that of the early Iron I villages, on the basis of which Gottwald in particular has argued for the distinctive polity and ideology of 'liberated Israel'.[12] Many of the social and economic mechanisms described by Gottwald, which for him imply an 'Israel' which did not exist when he imagines it to have, might still fit, insofar as they are valid, this later period–in particular, the institution of the *bêt 'abôt*, which Weinberg has argued as an innovation of the Persian period, pointing to a deliberate reconstitution of social groupings, a 'tribalization' which, like all tribalizations (including Gottwald's), is not ethnic nor primary, but economic and secondary.[13] There is no

---

10   P. Briant, 'Villages et communautés villageoises d'Asie achéménide et hellénistique', *Journal for Economic and Social History of the Orient*, 18 (1975), pp. 165-88; 'Appareils d'état et développement des forces productives au moyen-orient ancien: le cas de l'empire achéménide', *La Pensée*, February 1981, pp. 475-89.

11   'The Achaemenid Context', p. 66.

12   *The Tribes of Yahweh*, pp. 237-341.

13   See J. Weinberg, 'Das BEIT ABOTH im 6.-4. Jh. v. u. Z.,' *VT*  23 (1973),

reason why the obviously artificial twelve-tribe grouping of the biblical literature has to be connected with a social system of half a millennium earlier rather than one more recent.

More archaeological data relevant to Yehud dates to the mid-fifth century BCE. At this time a chain of fortresses was constructed, running from the Mediterranean to the Jordan, and down into the Negev, following the major trade routes of the region.[14] It seems unlikely that these were protecting borders; rather, they, and others like them elsewhere in the region, follow trade routes. Hoglund suggests that during the mid-fifth century an intensification of the Persian military presence occurred in response to the challenge of Greece on the Mediterranean seaboard and the contingent trade routes. There were Persian garrisons at both Arad and Beersheba, and Hoglund suggests a 'militarization' of Yehud, in the light of which the mission of Nehemiah might be understood.

Further light on the social organization of Yehud in the Persian period might be sought by focussing on another aspect of this society, namely its temple. The social and economic function of temples in the ancient Near East has been extensively studied in recent years[15] and there is evidence from both Babylonia and Egypt that the Achaemenid kings took care to rebuild local cult centres. How these cult-centres may have functioned, not only as a religious but also as an economic and political focus, has been suggested by the application of a distinct social model, called[16] a Bürger-Tempel-Gemeinde. Basically, such a social unit arises from a union between temple personnel and land owners, and creates a relatively autonomous economic system. A number of case-histories from Asia Minor, and from a slightly later

pp. 400-14.

14   See further on these fortresses E. Stern, *Material Culture of the Land of the Bible in the Persian Period*, Warminster: Aris and Phillips, 1982, p. 250; Hoglund, 'The Achaemenid Context,' pp. 63-4.

15   In particular by M.A. Dandamaev on Mesopotamia; see e.g. his 'Achaemenid Babylonia' in I.M. Diakonoff (ed.), *Ancient Mesopotamia. Socio-Economic History: A Collection of Studies by Soviet Scholars*, Moscow: Nuaka, 1969, pp. 296-311. For a recent discussion of the possible fucntion of the temple in Achaemenid Yehud, see J. Blenkinsopp, 'Temple and Society in Achaemenid Judah', *Second Temple Studies*, pp. 22-53.

16   On the origin of this term, coined by Soviet scholars, see Blenkinsopp, 'Temple and Society in Achaemenid Judah,' p. 27, n.1.

period, have been adduced. Many of the components of this sort of society, however, can be seen as present much earlier; in Mesopotamia the temple owned and administered a great deal of land (owned by the deity), acted as a treasury for its city, its priests often exercising a civic authority. Thus, what Weinberg sees as a fairly distinct form of social organization, Blenkinsopp understands as a variation on a common pattern.

In the absence of any of the kinds of contemporary texts which illuminate the structure and workings of ancient Near Eastern temple-economies (other than lists of produce and officials), we can only inferentially describe what is called 'Second Temple' Judaean society.[17] The one critical feature of the Bürger-Tempel-Gemeinde, however, is that it posits a society *within* a society, a privileged group with restricted membership, not co-extensive with the wider society of the province as a whole. Such an exclusive society does in fact seem to be indicated in the book of Nehemiah, where it is termed the $q^e hal$ *haggōlâ* and its members the $b^e n\hat{e}$ *haggōlâ,* who exclude the native population on grounds of ethnic and cultic impurity and undertake both the rebuild and thereafter to control the Temple–and thus to regulate the economy.

This society, the theory runs, over time extended itself so that eventually it included the whole of Yehud. A slightly different view, argued by Morton Smith,[18] sees two groups of exiles returning: members of the 'Yahweh-alone' party and descendants of the former Jerusalem priesthood. The former call themselves the $b^e n\hat{e}$ *haggōlâ.* The two groups were in opposition to the resident population, who are

17    It is particularly puzzling that the biblical literature, for whom the temple is such an important institution, contains no description of the 'second Temple' itself nor of its actual building, apart from Hab. 1.14. There is a clear admission in Hag. 2.3 that this hasty (?) effort produced nothing in comparison to the former building. But is this historically correct, or does this verse merely assume that the previous sanctuary *must* have been bigger? Perhaps, as far as the remainder of the biblical literature is concerned, it was the continuity with the first Temple that needed to be stressed, and thus the (hypothesized) 'original' building won precedence over the construction of the contemporary one. We cannot really assert with much confidence when the Jerusalem temple of the Persian period was erected or how far it amounted to a restoration of the earlier one. Nor, of course, can we assert that it was the only Yahwistic temple built at this time.

18    *Palestinian Parties*, pp. 75-112.

referred to as the 'people of the land'. Nehemiah was a tyrant (in the strict sense) and secured for the 'Yahweh-alone' party control of the Temple and thus of the society. The place of Ezra in modern reconstructions is best left out because there is uncertainty as to whether he came before Nehemiah, after, or whether he came at all.[19] However, Blenkinsopp has brought to light a parallel to the mission with which Ezra seems to have been entrusted. A certain Udjahorresnet, an Egyptian priest, was sent back to Egypt by Darius I to reorganize the priestly 'houses of life', i.e. the scribal schools, which, in Blenkinsopp's view, must have included the regulation of the cult.[20] It is known that Darius had the traditional Egyptian law codified and written up in Aramaic and demotic Egyptian.[21]

What has been reviewed in the preceding paragraphs suggest two things. First, the 'restoration' of the province of Yehud was the result of a deliberate Persian policy, namely a strategy to reorganize the empire. This reorganization seems to have included the resettlement of peoples, the foundation of new settlements, the restoration/creation of temples, and sometimes the establishment of lawcodes. The combined effect of these three initiatives in the case of Yehud/Judah is to create a society the core of which has been brought into the land from outside, which is organizing itself on what it sees as a traditional cult around a temple, and which is constituted as a new ethnic entity. The circumstances which both the non-biblical evidence indicates and the biblical account of Nehemiah and Ezra confirms provide the earliest plausible context for the creation of the biblical 'Israel': the 'ethnic' collectives, the exclusive 'exile'-society, and the provision of a central sanctuary and a law.

19   There is hardly a need to document the discussion, merely to note that the view of C.C. Torrey, *Ezra Studies*, Chicago: University of Chicago Press, 1910, that Ezra was a fictional character has been revived by Garbini (*History and Ideology*, pp. 151-69).

20   On the 'house of life' see R.J. Williams, 'The Sage in Egyptian Literature', in J.G. Gammie and L. Perdue (eds), *The Sage in Israel and the Ancient Near East*, Winona Lake: Eisenbrauns, 1990, pp. 19-30 (27-29).

21   On Persian lawmaking, see J. Blenkinsopp, *A History of Prophecy in Israel: From the Settlement in the Land to the Hellenistic Period*, Philadelphia: Westminster, 1983, p. 227; A.T. Olmstead, 'Darius as Lawgiver', *AJSL* 51 (1935), 247-49 and *History of the Persian Empire*, Chicago: University of Chicago Press, 1948, pp. 119-342.

The danger here, perhaps, is of falling into the methodological trap that I so strenuously criticized earlier, namely of using the biblical story as a framework for reconstructing history. Indeed, I wonder whether many scholarly reconstructions of this Persian society do not lend too much credence to the books of Ezra and Nehemiah. Given the well-known historical muddle and the complicated and as yet unresolved issues of their literary history, one might well wish to accord to these narratives rather less historical value than is usual. The objection is sound and technically correct, and one must, I think, avoid the charge of switching from scepticism to credulity concerning the biblical literature once it has passed the sixth century BCE! There is no particular reason to assume that the process of idealization, the creation of ideal situations and entities, has been abandoned by the writers of these books. However, with the necessary caution afforded, two considerations can be brought to bear on this case. One is that, unlike the case with Iron Age 'Israel', the non-biblical data does to a degree afford confirmation of some of the basic processes described in the biblical narrative at this point. Another is that processes of the kind described in Ezra and Nehemiah would seem to be necessitated by the subsequent developments in the emergence of Judaean society and its religion. In other words, there is no problem created by a conflict of literary and archaeological data, nor are the processes described unable to explain the later development of the culture of the province.

Nevertheless, to grant this much is not to assert that the figures of Nehemiah and Ezra are fully historical (the latter perhaps not historical at all), and certainly not that either achieved all that is credited to him. It is very likely that gradual processes have been foreshortened and ascribed to certain individuals, following the laws of narrative dramatization. It remains valid, nonetheless, to propose on the basis of the biblical *and* non-biblical data that the social conditions appropriate for the emergence of the biblical Israel are to be found in Persian period Yehud. Perhaps we can even distinguish stages in the process. The Persian reconstitution of Yehud divides into three major initiatives, one (economic, agricultural) dating from the end of the sixth century, under Cyrus or more probably Darius I, another (military) in the mid-fifth century (Xerxes) and a third (legal, constitutional) in the late sixth or early fifth century. In the biblical narrative, these roughly correspond to the 'return of the exiles', and the missions of Nehemiah and Ezra. The major respect in which the biblical account *differs* from what is implied by the non-biblical evidence is that the reconstruction of Yehud was brought about by the 'exiles' of 'Israel',[22] i.e. a Judaean initiative, and that it reconstituted the culture that had once been there before. It is true that according to the books of Ezra and Nehemiah the 'return' is authorized, and assisted, by Cyrus, together with the restoration of the cult and sanctuary of Yhwh. Nehemiah 2, however, ascribes the initiative for his mission to Nehemiah, not Artaxerxes. The Persians remain liberators and restorers in these accounts, and necessarily so if the theme of continuity with the past is to be played.

### The creation of an idealized Israel in Yehud

To explain the existence of the biblical literature, we must conclude that the creation of what was in truth a *new* society, marking a definitive break with what had preceded, was accompanied by–or at least soon generated–an ideological superstructure which denied its more recent origins, its imperial basis, and instead indigenized itself. Its literate class (within the $g\bar{o}l\hat{a}$-society) created an identity continuous with kingdoms that had previously occupied that area, of whom no doubt some concrete memory remained within Palestine, and very probably some archival material too, and wrote into the history of their region an 'Israel' which explained their own post-'exilic' society and the rights and privileges of the immigrant élite within that society. This process did not occur suddenly, nor was it ever entirely coherently accomplished. But the end product formed the major part of what we now know as the biblical literature.

Let us assess the main ingredients of the biblical 'Israel' in the context of this new society. First, the 'exile' is, if not a myth in the sense of an event that did not occur, then at least an interpretation of a transportation out of, and later a transportation into, Judah which turned historical discontinuity into continuity. In that respect the exile is the central myth of the biblical account of the past. The immigrants, like the Pilgrim Fathers, had their minority experience come to

22   It is still worth remembering, however, that the details of the story were not always accurately remembered. Thus, 2 Maccabees seems to think that it was the Persians who exiled 'our fathers' (1.19), while Nebuchadnezzar is made king of the Assyrians in Judith (1.1; 4.1).

determine the identity of the majority whose real history was different. However, this central paradox, by which the immigrants displaced the indigenous, manifested itself in other narratives too, celebrating an original 'Israel' that was brought into the 'promised land' from outside, and distinguished itself radically and polemically from the indigenous population. There are in the biblical literature several such stories of origin, including the stories of Abraham, the Exodus and the conquest.

But the biblical myth of Israelite origins in Palestine does not have 'Israel' displacing the 'Canaanites' entirely; they remain in the land. This was of course the case in Persian Yehud. In Ezra-Nehemiah we encounter the 'people of the land' who are characterized as impure and of alien stock, with whom the true 'Israel' is not to mingle its 'holy seed.' It is these–perhaps those outside the *gōlâ*-society, or outside the newly established communes and their emergent 'tribes'?– who become in Genesis–Kings the 'Canaanites', of whom very much the same is said. In each case we find antagonism towards the indigenous population, and separation from it, a separation based on the principles of ethnicity and religious adherence to the true ancestral cult.

And then there is the relationship between Yehud and Samaria. The story of Nehemiah portrays a rivalry between the two centres, Samaria being the more important at first in the context of the Persian empire, Jerusalem being the place of the temple chosen by the 'god of Israel'. Yet again, the parallel in the Genesis–Kings history is the schism between Israel and Judah, in which Israel is presented as a defecting (and defective) branch of the true 'Israel' whose religion is focussed on Jerusalem. This account, unlike that of Nehemiah, also betrays a claim on behalf of Judah over the territory of Samaria. Several scholars find in Chronicles a similar concern to embrace the territory of Samaria within the same orbit as Judah. Possibly behind this lies some historical substance. Since it is certain that the inhabitants of the region of Samaria worshipped Yhwh (whether or not exclusively) the issue of explaining this fact and acting upon it must have arisen. The same is true of the Transjordanian territories where also numbers of Yhwh worshippers seem to have been found. Possibly the same is even true of Edom. The problem is tackled initially in Genesis–Kings by means of genealogical codes: Ammon and Moab are descended from Abraham's father (through Lot), and

Edom from Isaac (through Esau); the inhabitants of Samaria from Jacob.

Finally, there is the covenant. A covenant ceremony lies at the heart of the Ezra–Nehemiah narrative, and historically such a religious ritual and theological theory may well have its origin at this time in a community constitution linking a society and a God and a sanctuary. If the book of Deuteronomy could be plausibly dated to the pre-'exilic' period, we would be obliged to allow an earlier origin. But the social situation which Deuteronomy envisages is more consistent with the post-monarchic situation, with justice administered *de jure* and not just *de facto* by elders, a virtually absent monarch, and a society governed by a lawcode. Indeed, the paraenetic character of Deuteronomy, so well explained by von Rad[23] has a counterpart in the description in Nehemiah 8.7-8 of the reading of the law and its explanation by Levites. It is also the Deuteronomic ideology which exhibits the Canaanites and their religious practices in the way I have earlier discussed. No simpler or more important single step in reorientating biblical scholarship on the history of Israel exists than relocating Deuteronomy to a much more likely setting in the sixth or fifth century BCE. From that none single move, a great deal else follows with relative ease.

Not all elements of the mythic complex created by this society serve such deep problems of self-identity. Some serve to compensate for political and economic impotence by exploiting the freedom to write out a fictional past in glorious tones. A wonderful example of this, in a nutshell, might be offered as a replacement for von Rad's famous 'kleines Credo'. In Ezra 4.19ff. is a decree ascribed to the Persian king, which many scholars still think is authentic. Artaxerxes is supposed to have written as follows:

> And I made a decree, and search has been made, and it has been found that this city from of old has risen against kings, and that rebellion and sedition have been made in it. And mighty kings have been over Jerusalem, who ruled over the whole province of Beyond the River to whom tribute, custom and toll were paid...

Well, I have argued that the claim about kings in Jerusalem ruling over such a huge area is historically untrue, and therefore it must follow that nothing such as is reported here could have appeared in records available to Artaxerxes. It is hardly possible that the king

---

23   G. von Rad, *Studies in Deuteronomy* (SBT, 9), London: SCM Press, 1953.

fabricated the case as a pretext for his decision; the Persian kings did not need excuses for what they did, least of all false ones. No: the decree does not come from Artaxerxes at all. There is no decree. Rather, by the time that this piece of fiction was written, the history of what is to become the biblical Israel was well under way: the clerks of the Ministry of History in Yehud were already claiming their tiny province to be the relic of a once mighty empire, indeed claiming some kind of jurisdiction over the entire satrapy (or half-satrapy) of 'Beyond the River', the land promised to Abraham in Genesis and ruled over by David and Solomon. Was it perhaps on the basis of this fictional claim, which a Persian king, no less, has been made to endorse (a clever move to have this endorsement a reason for a decree hostile to Yehud!) that later Judaean kings, the Hasmonaeans, set about recreating what they believed to be the boundaries of historical Israel, including in their scope those kindred 'half-Jews' from Idumaea and Transjordan?

To be sure, the biblical literature is not completely consistent in fulfilling its overall aims. Authors are authors and not all the Judaean scribes were hacks. Within the scribal institutions different authors advanced their own favoured notions and perspectives. Williamson[24] has recently examined variations in the portrayal of 'Israel' with respect to Samaria. Thus in his view, in Ezekiel Israel is 'a single people of God', while Jeremiah maintains a difference between 'Israel' and 'Judah'. Deutero-Isaiah uses 'Israel' mostly in apposition to 'Jacob' and apparently referring to the exiles (or, in the case of 49.1-6 a portion of the exiles), while Trito-Isaiah betrays little tension between various communities claiming to be 'Israel'. With Ezra, an ethnic definition is introduced, that of the 'holy seed', which should not mix with the 'people of the land'. Despite the Chronicler's attempts at reconciliation, allowing a place for 'assimilationists' but insisting on the priority of the Temple, the tensions now prevalent led to the formation of schisms, leading to the formation of the Samaritan community and other groups.

Williamson is describing what he regards as a concept 'in transition', having already a history in monarchic times. However, it would be truer to speak of the concept 'in creation'; although the name 'Israel' and its attachment to a former kingdom (and possibly its

---

24 H.G.M. Willliamson, 'The Concept of Israel in Transition,' in R.E. Clements (ed.), *The World of Ancient Israel*, Cambridge: CUP, 1989, pp. 141-159.

use by a remaining population in Samaria) are preconditions, the concept of which Williamson is speaking is already ethnic and religious. It is more probable that we have in the biblical literature cited by Williamson indications of the way in which the formation of the idea of 'Israel' embraced different projects before its more or less stable form in the Genesis–Kings account was achieved. However, let us beware of assuming a particular chronological sequence among the biblical literature. That, too, belongs to a former way of thinking. For the time being, at least, at the level at which we are dealing, which is fairly general, we need only think of this literature as simultaneous, with a few obvious exceptions. But that does not make it entirely homogeneous.

Thus, although the same ideological momentum is common to all the literature, the details can differ. In his discussion of origin stories during this period, H. Tadmor reaches similar conclusions about the concepts of Israel.[25] Tadmor notes that a number of different accounts of origins exists in the biblical literature, some of which make Israel invaders or immigrants from elsewhere, and yet some which make them indigenous. It may be speculated that the tension between these two reflects a struggle between two groups, in which the minority view of the genuinely indigenous makes its voice heard. But equally, it may not. The existence of these conflicting ideas implies that there is no single authoritative or 'official' account of the origins of Israel permeating all the literature. The more coherent and larger-scale compositions such as Genesis–Kings (or Genesis–Deuteronomy and Joshua–Kings) have not obliterated other accounts elsewhere in the corpus. Hostility for Edom conflicts with recognition of brotherhood; Jonah and Ruth and Esther and Tamar all point to either diverging ideologies or perhaps debate within a wider governing ideology. The divergence does not need to be explained by the perpetuation of older 'traditions'; this procedure solves nothing and merely pushes the problem one stage further back. It is more economical an explanation,

25  H. Tadmor, 'The Origins of Israel as Seen in the Exilic and Post-Exilic Ages', in *Le Origini di Israele*, Rome: Accademia Nazionale dei Lincei, 1987, pp. 15-27. The oft-quoted accusation of Ezek. 16.3,45 that Canaan is the land of Israel's ancestry may betray knowledge of an indigenous origin, though it seems to me equally likely that this is a polemic against the myth of extra-territorial origin rather than a deliberate statement of fact, effectively saying that Israel's behaviour makes it unworthy of its distinctive origin.

and I think more historically plausible as well, that these different strands are in simultaneous competition, and perhaps not always consciously if their authors are unaware of the alternatives.[26] The established view of the origins of Israel is not determined prior to the writing, but emerges out of it, without having effaced all trace of contradictory views. In other words, the conflicting accounts of Israel's origins point to a situation in which the definition of the 'ideal' Israel was in process of being formed.

Not every major biblical myth makes the best possible sense in the light of the conditions implied in the books of Ezra and Nehemiah, and indeed some may be later. But cumulatively, an impressive case can be made for the fifth century BCE as the time and Yehud as the place for formation of what biblical scholars call the 'biblical tradition', and what can more simply and accurately be called the biblical literature

And now to a final consideration. If we are right to see in the biblical literature the fruits of a process of ideological expression which has its roots in the society of Persian period Yehud/Judah, we must nevertheless beware of the habit of biblical scholars of pretending to more knowledge than we have. The description we have of that society represents the viewpoint of an élite. The society of Yehud as depicted and implied (I think of Chronicles as an example of transparent implication) in the biblical literature differs from the depiction of the biblical Israel only in that it is a portrait of a real society and not an imagined one. But the portrait is just as ideological. The 'exile' that dominates the story of monarchic Israel has its counterpart in the 'restoration' of 'post-exilic' Israel. Ezra and Nehemiah present this 'restored' society as the remnant of the biblical Israel, and indeed that is how we must insist on viewing it, as a literary construct.

But the society which these writings claim to describe is in no sense an Israel, historically speaking. It is a Persian province with the name of Yehud or Yehudah (Judah). It is reconstituted on the territory of the erstwhile kingdom of Judah, and it enshrines the cult of the god Yahweh. The connection between this society and Israel is this: the scribal class of this new society creates an identity and heritage for itself in Palestine, an identity expressed in a vigorous and remarkably

---

26   Though, as John Rogerson commented on reading this, the books of Jonah and Ruth can be interpreted in the light of a conscious debate on this issue.

coherent (all things considered) literary corpus. That identity is given the name 'Israel' (which now exists alongside Judah). The society itself, or more accurately, parts of that society, will transform itself in the direction of becoming the 'Israel' of its own creation as it accepts that Israel's presumed history as its own, accepts its constitution, beliefs and habits as its own, and begins to incarnate that identity. That, as I see it, is the relationship of the authors of the biblical literature to Israel. but before considering how that process of incarnation began to develop (and it never can or will achieve definitive incarnation), we can indulge in some reconstruction of the character of these creators of Israel and their place and methods of work. Having answered in a very general and preliminary way the question 'why was the Bible written?' it is time to look more closely at how and by whom, in aid of which we shall have to deploy a little imagination.

Chapter Six

WHO WROTE THE BIBLICAL LITERATURE,
AND WHERE?

In the previous chapter I brought to and end the first part of the argument of this book, which suggested that the society which grew up in Yehud in the Persian period is the matrix for the production of the biblical Israel. In other words, I proposed in effect a redefinition of the 'biblical period'. But I had to acknowledge that of the history of this period we know too little to be able to reconstruct in much detail how the biblical literature was actually composed. In this chapter I am nevertheless attempting to establish with a little more precision the circumstances in which I believe this literature *must* have been written, and to offer an idea of the *kind* of institutional context in which the older-established literary-critical methods of biblical criticism, such as source-criticism, redaction-criticism and tradition-criticism might reorientate themselves away from a notion of 'ancient Israel' and its 'traditions'.

*Sources*

It is important at the outset for me to repeat that although the *ideological structure* of the biblical literature can only be explained in the last analysis as a product of the Persian period, it need not follow that all the *content* of this literature arose only at this time. A certain amount of material, in the form of pieces of written or of oral literature–for example, stories about kings, warriors and holy men, songs cultic and non-cultic must have survived in Palestine. Likewise, domestic and social customs, cultic and legal practices will have persisted from the Iron Age into the Persian period. In analyzing the biblical literature the use of such pre-existing sources must obviously be allowed for, and not simply where such sources are evident. But mere antiquity is not the point; it is a kind of reflex in biblical scholarship that antiquity is in some way an index of historical value or authenticity. However, if what I have argued in the previous chapters is correct, then these older relics, whatever they are, cannot be ascribed to 'ancient Israel'. They emerge from a society about which we know fairly little, the society of the old kingdoms of Israel or of Judah. What we cannot do with any of these relics is to carry back with them into their antiquity the social and religious context with which they have been provided by the writers of the biblical literature, who are creating their own literary 'Israel'. They are not relics of what is often loosely called the 'biblical society'. I cannot emphasize strongly enough the importance of this distinction, since it is on this point that I am most likely to be misunderstood or misrepresented. The issue is not about the geographical or temporal provenance of material in the biblical literature: it is about the essential incompatibility of the historical Israel (and Judah) with the biblical construct, and hence the difference between the society of historical Israel and the society which created the biblical Israel. This latter society is born only in the Persian period, and in that sense the biblical literature, as opposed to relics which it incorporated and re-formed and re-contextualized, is a product of what we call the Second Temple Period.

A more intriguing question is the source-material that may have derived from the culture of the immigrants. Much of the narrative in Genesis 1–11 may reflect such origins (as is acknowledged readily for what has been assigned to 'P', though less readily for 'J'), and quite probably a good deal of legal material as well. The cult of a high god, a phenomenon which arises from time to time in the ancient Near East and which manifested itself in Nabonidus's embrace of Sin,[1] then in the Zoroastrian religion of the Achaemenids,[2] is obviously presupposed in the biblical literature, though whether we find monotheism any more than in these other cults is a moot point; rather

1   For texts of Nabonidus, see *ANET*, pp. 560-62.

2   The affiliation of the early Achaemenids to Zoroastrianism is probable, though disputed. See, in favour, M. Boyce, *A History of Zoroastrianism*, Leiden: Brill, 1975 and her 'Persian Religion in the Achemenid Age', in *CHJ* 1, pp. 279-307; for a review of this and other questions relating to Zoroastrianism and the biblical literature, see E. Yamauchi, *Persia and the Bible*, Grand Rapids: Baker Book House, 1990. A rather minimal view of later connections between Persian religion and Judaism is given in S. Shaked, 'Iranian Influence on Judaism: First Century B.C.E. to Second Century B.C.E', *CHJ* 1, pp.308-25.

we have a case of syncretism, in which various deities are identified with one (Yahweh, Elohim, Shaddai, Elyon, El). Babylon, in the Neo-Babylonian and Persian periods is a more likely place of origin for this kind of cult than Iron Age Palestine, where it is not attested.[3] But the extent to which the 'biblical religion' derives from immigrants that the Persians brought from Mesopotamia into Yehud is only one of a number of implication of my overall argument which will have to be left for another study. But in the sense just defined, it would still be correct to say, as biblical scholarship has always maintained, that the 'biblical religion' was in most essentials the contribution of those whom the biblical literature calls the 'exiles'.

## *The theological view of biblical origins*

Naturally, I am advocating  a quite different perception of the formation of the biblical literature from what is current. It may be helpful at this point to remind ourselves of what view is taken of the origin of the biblical literature by the vast majority of scholars who have written on the subject. The question of how the biblical literature was created has been answered, in general terms, by sketching out a long process of evolution. The earliest stages, in most cases, are posited as oral 'traditions' which were in the course of time written down, edited (often several times) and finally reached their present shape–more or less, since the history of the textual forms shows fluidity long after the basic shape of the scroll is fixed. On this view, the end-product is not clearly foreseen at the outset: biblical scrolls just came to be the way they are by a natural evolution. The process of 'transmission' is treated as if it were almost automatic. What is oral will become written; what is written will be faithfully copied by scribes; but equally 'faith'-fully will it at times be recast by redactors.

3    H. Niehr has published a study of the process by which a 'high god' emerges in the religion of Syria and Palestine, which he very plausibly compares to the emergence of Yhwh in Judah (*Der höchste Gott: Alttestamentlicher JHWH-Glaube im Kontext syrisch-kanaanäischer Religion des 1. Jahrtausends v. Chr.* (BZAW, 190), Berlin: De Gruyter, 1990). Although he attributes much less to Persian influence than I do, his study documents the Persian-Hellenistic period ( see his sources!) as the period in which this process can be discerned. In any event, it is an important gain, from the historian's point of view, to be able to see and understand the biblical 'monotheism' (or whatever term is appropriate) not as a unique and thus historically inaccessible phenomenon, but as part of a wider pattern of religious evolution in Syria-Palestine.

The whole process is generally called 'tradition' and most students of biblical 'traditions' assume that at every point we have a sort of coherent statement, sometimes amounting to a living expression of the 'faith of Israel' which issues finally in that definitive canon, the Bible. Biblical scholarship recognizes that the literature evolved: there was not always a canon as we have inherited it. But by way of compensation we have either a 'tradition' or a 'canonizing process' which merely changes what is a synchronic (canon) into a diachronic (canonical process) perspective.

The evolution of the Bible, then, tends to be presented by a great number of biblical scholars as if analogous to that of a human being, in which some kind of religious/literary/social DNA code determines the final form of the individual person. In this way, 'critical' study of the biblical literature achieves a history of Israel's 'faith', but at the same time redeems its 'critical', 'historical' approach theologically. In language which thoroughly confuses the historical and theological, Israel's 'faith' shapes the 'formation' of its 'tradition'. As a result, although the theology of the Bible is not exactly equated with the religion of ancient Israel (though this happens surprisingly often, as I showed earlier), the biblical 'traditions' produced by biblical scholarship can be directly related to the 'faith' (='religion') of 'Israel': the religion of Israel is the history of the biblical 'traditions.'

But quite apart from the non-existence of the 'Israel' in question, this explanation assumes that the Bible in some way represents the religious beliefs of a social group, and this is clearly not so.[4] Neither rabbinic Judaism nor Christianity in fact regarded the Bible as comprising 'the faith of Israel'. Both came to appeal to it in support of their own beliefs, and regarded it as revelation from God. Both religions appealed to the literature as in some way authoritative,[5] but never was it seen as expressing the religious faith of an actual historical community–and rightly, since it never did, nor could it have, since it is ideologically diverse and even self-contradictory. Its deity abhors and delights in sacrifice, believes and disbelieves in retribution, contains differing accounts of the same historical incidents, and so on. It is scholars who have, in trying to salvage

4    See J. Barr, 'Judaism–Its Continuity with the Bible', *The 7th Montefiore Memorial Lecture*, University of Southampton, 1968.
5    In the case of rabbinic Judaism, this occurred when midrash began to supplement mishnah and culminated in the Babylonian Talmud; in the case of Christianity, scripture achieved a comparable status only with the Reformers.

theological merit from historical criticism, converted it into something that they believe has both historical *and* theological authority!

But the Bible came about as the result of canonization, and thus began to operate in distinct ways within the communities that canonized it. It has never been proven, and is intrinsically unlikely, that the *idea* of a canon preceded a canon itself. Blenkinsopp has rightly complained that this issue has failed to be seen as a sociological rather than a religious one.[6] The origin of the biblical literature cannot be concealed under the blanket of 'Israel's faith'. Besides, 'Israel's faith' historically, is a meaningless concept; even 'Israel's religion' begs a large number of questions. The study of early Judaism shows that much of its belief and practice actually has no counterpart in the biblical literature (the Mishnah, Enoch, the Dead Sea Scrolls all endorse this statement). The process whereby the biblical writings came to form an essential core of Jewish and Christian belief is much later than the time of writing of the literature. The biblical literature does form, as some theologians imply or assert, a bridge between ancient and modern 'communities of faith'; rather it is a watershed, and only on our side, since a certain moment in time, is the Bible a Bible; before this moment in which it was created as a Bible, its nature and its relationship as literature to its authors and its society are different and remain to be clarified.

### The Society

Abandoning the view just outlined, let us return to the point where this chapter began: the formation of a corpus of literature which comes to be the Bible starts within the society created in Judah in the Persian period. What constituted this society, and, specifically, what elements in this constitution provoked the need for the creation of this quite unusual corpus?

6     J. Blenkinsopp, *Prophecy and Canon. A Contribution to the Study of Jewish Origins*, Notre Dame, University of Notre Dame Press, 1977, p. 147-48: 'One of the most pressing needs in biblical studies is for a thoroughly competent sociological examination of the phenomena which specialists in the field tend to look at only from the religious perspective. The idea of a canon, in particular, would call for examination as an aspect of social history, implying as it does claims to authority and comprehensive attempts at legitimation on the part of different groups and individuals.'

The predominant biblical view is that this society was a restoration of exiles from 'pre-exilic' Judah, and this view is, as I argued in the previous chapter, partly correct. The Persians did seek to redevelop the province economically and culturally. To that end they transported people into Yehud. But what cultural background did these immigrants bring with them? The biblical story wishes to persuade us of a mass migration of 'Israel' to Babylon, leaving an empty land[7] and later returning with the original 'law of Moses'. To their literary baggage scholars have wanted to add further large chunks of the Bible, including the 'Deuteronomistic History', 'J', 'P', Jeremiah and much else, a good deal of it written in Babylonia. However, surviving literature of the monarchic period, as Martin Noth quite correctly insisted,[8] will surely have remained in Palestine, and not have been removed to Babylon. It is among those dismissed by the biblical narrative as the unworthy 'peoples of the land' who will have been responsible for preserving whatever was left to them (and, in Noth's view, actually composing the 'Deuteronomistic History').

But whether in Babylon or in Palestine, such literary activity presupposes exactly what I have challenged: that the biblical 'Israel' was an historical entity from whom the appropriate 'traditions' were 'received' and transmitted little altered. But as it is, not only have we to acknowledge that a great deal of creative literary activity must postdate the Iron Age, including the Deuteronomistic History, the Chronicler, Ezra–Nehemiah, Ezekiel, Jeremiah, much or most of Isaiah, Haggai, Zechariah, Jonah, Esther, Daniel, Ecclesiastes, Lamentations, Malachi, the recension of the Pentateuch; there is in addition no *necessity* to assign *any* part of the formation of *any* biblical book to the period.of the historical kingdoms of Judah and Israel. Here, of course, I am excluding relics from this earlier period, as I indicated at the beginning of this chapter. The existence of such relics is not, on my definition, part of the literary process any more than the existence of chaos is part of the process of creation. Since it is already clear that a great deal of literary activity must have taken place in the Persian–Hellenistic period, it seems more reasonable to insist on arguments for an earlier dating rather than, as in current (but, to be fair, increasingly violated) practice, to date as much as

---

7    For an examination of this ideology, see R.P. Carroll, 'Textual Strategies and Ideology in the Second Temple Period', in *Second Temple Studies*, pp. 108-24.

8    M. Noth, *The History of Israel*, pp. 289-93.

possible as early as possible and require strong evidence for 'later' dating.

At all events, other than Psalm 137 there is no literature in the Bible with an ostensibly 'exilic' setting, and nothing except Lamentations with an ostensible setting in post-destruction Jerusalem.[9] Certainly, structures of thought and of social organization which could have an origin in an exilic setting have been identified;[10] the problem in deciding for or against such elements, however, persists in the fact that the situation in Persian period Yehud, of which we know as little, if not less, than we do of the deported communities in Babylon, may well have been such as to create similar cultural symptoms! Thus, the influence of Babylonian mythological themes and motifs in Genesis 1–11, Isaiah 40–55 and Ezekiel, which have often been interpreted as indications of exilic origin, are just as likely in a Judaean community which included many newly-arrived immigrants from Mesopotamia (although it is likely that these stories were known in Palestine from 1000 BCE to the Greco-Roman period and beyond!) To these elements ought to be added others absorbed from the indigenous Palestinian religious culture.[11]

There are two other considerations to be dealt with before we go further. It has long been taken for granted in biblical scholarship, in defence of its view summarized above, that the biblical literature evolved over a fairly long period of time, and source-critical, redactional-critical and traditio-critical analyses have assumed such a long time-scale and elaborated the process of development in accordance with this longevity. The impression is easily gained, from reading biblical scholarship, that the literature cannot have begun its history as late as the Persian period, since the processes of tradition-formation discerned in it, the many redactions, glosses, and so on, need time to have evolved. This impression can be safely discarded. The process by which books are copied in the ancient world, where every individual copy *is* literally a newly-created scribal artifact, and where every copy can be as faithful or as deviant as the scribe or his

9 The setting of parts of Ezekiel and Jeremiah between 596 and 586 is only a marginal exception. I owe to John Rogerson the keen observation that the word 'there' in Ps. 137.1 actually shows it to have been composed elsewhere.

10 One of the best attempts at such an analysis is D. Smith, *The Religion of the Landless*, Bloomington: Meyer-Stone, 1989.

11 As argued by Niehr, *Der höchste Gott*, who uses the name 'Canaanite' for the indigenous culture.

patron determines, can quickly generate not only the multiplicity of textual forms to which the Qumran biblical manuscripts attest, but also the rapid appearance of different 'recensions'. A conscientious and hard-working scribe in a lifetime of copying could very easily create a 'Deuteronomistic' version of everything that passed through his hands; the interests of an individual patron by whom a copy was commissioned could well induce a clear ideological bias or concern within that copy. The *phenomena* of redactions, glosses, and other expansions which the biblical scholar sees in a text may be genuine: the existence of 'schools', 'circles' and 'traditions' is part of the theory, not the evidence. The analysis by McKane of the composition of Jeremiah as a 'rolling corpus'[12] is instructive: for all the intricacies of transmission which this analysis detects, the *terminus a quo* is the lifetime of Jeremiah, perhaps three generations before the establishment of the society of Yehud. Some decades earlier, Martin Noth had argued that the process of formation of the Pentateuchal tradition was substantially complete already before the formation of the Israelite state–and all in oral form![13] The whole discipline of tradition-history has been skewed by the assumption of pre-exilic compositions and collections and redactions, dictated by belief in the biblical 'history' of 'Israel'. The Dead Sea Scrolls show that quite complex literary developments can occur over an apparently short period of time.[14] In any case, proof is not lacking that 'traditions' can develop extremely quickly, and like all other stories come into being by a process of invention.[15]

12   W. McKane, *Jeremiah* (ICC), Edinburgh: T. and T. Clark, 1986, pp. l-lxxxiii.

13   M. Noth, *A History of Pentateuchal Traditions*, ET Englewood Cliffs: Prentice-Hall, 1972, p. 45.

14   I am thinking of the examples of the *War Scroll*, of which we have a fairly complete (?) copy from Cave 1 which is obviously compiled from various older sources, but which, as fragments from Cave 4 show, existed in other, earlier forms; and to the *Temple Scroll*, also a compilation of sources, some of these themselves compilations. For the relevant evidence and argumentation see my *1QM, The War Scroll from Qumran*, Rome, 1977 and Michael O. Wise, *A Critical Study of the The Temple Scroll from Qumran Cave 11* (SAOC, 49), Chicago: Oriental Institute, 1990.

15   The classic discussion and collection of such 'traditions' is by E. Hobsbawm and T. Ranger (eds.), *The Invention of Tradition*, Cambridge: CUP, 1983.

## 'Biblical Hebrew'

A more substantial problem is often thought to be the linguistic one. Analysis of biblical literature is frequently used to give relative dates to the biblical books; thus Ecclesiastes and Jonah are 'late', as is Chronicles, while 'P' and Ezekiel are 'exilic' and Deuteronomy 'pre-exilic'. It is customary to speak with confidence of 'Late Biblical Hebrew'. There can be no doubt that the biblical literature is linguistically varied. But interpreting this phenomenon is a different matter, and again it is controlled by an overall perspective which is false. First, there is extraordinarily little by way of external control on the dating of 'classical Hebrew', by which is usually meant the language of Deuteronomy or of 'J'; we have very few non-biblical texts by which to date the evolution of the language in which the biblical literature is written. Thus, in his well-known study of the language of P,[16] A. Hurvitz argues that it predates Ezekiel, and thus is pre-exilic. But this involves taking Ezekiel as datable to the 6th century. What linguistic criteria date Ezekiel to this time? The argument assumes that Ezekiel or a contemporary, is the author of the book, and this is not even a view sustained by many commentators on the book! What if Ezekiel were written a hundred years later than Hurvitz assumes? By what peg can Ezekiel itself be dated? It is curious how many scholars feel themselves able to discern differences in Hebrew between the 7th and 5th centuries BCE (i.e. 'pre-exilic' and 'post-exilic') but do not use linguistic arguments to determine whether the Yahwist wrote under David (putatively 10th century BCE) or during the exile four centuries later? *That* should be much easier to decide!

---

16　A. Hurvitz, 'The Evidence of Language in Dating the Priestly Code', *RB* 81 (1974), pp. 24-56. A fuller study of the language of Ezekiel by M. F. Rooker, *Biblical Hebrew in Transition: The Language of the Book of Ezekiel* (JSOTS, 90), Sheffield: JSOT Press, 1990, makes a distinction between changes due to natural evolution and those due to Aramaic influence. The latter can be ignored unless the influence of Aramaic on Hebrew was something that increased with time, or that must be present after a certain date; both premises are questionable. The former depends greatly on Polzin's work with Chronicles, though Rooker also rightly criticizes several of Polzin's criteria (pp. 36ff.). The same basic criticism applies to all this work, however: can we date enough biblical literature on non-linguistic grounds to avoid arguing in a circle?

An associated error is the confusion of typology[17] and chronology. That is to say, between usages which may be understood as being logically prior or posterior in terms of the general development of linguistic behaviour, and usages which are actually earlier or later in time. Thus, within the suburbs of Sheffield, I am not surprised to hear 'thee' and 'thy' being used by adults and children alike who live in certain nearby areas. I am aware that this usage is, in standard English obsolete, and so might be regarded as typologically older. It is, however, chronologically contemporary. This example should not be taken as more than illustrative of the point that typological analysis implies an *ideal* chronological sequence only. But we all know that languages do not in fact behave according to these ideal sequences; they evolve differently in different places and societies. The language I read is not even homogeneous: spoken English may be reproduced in a book alongside literary English, and the two are different. Dating biblical literature by its language is a useful exercise, but requires a certain sophistication.

It *may* be legitimate to conclude, for example, that the language of 'P' is *typologically* earlier than Ezekiel, but this does not necessarily mean that chronologically it is earlier. Among the Dead Sea Scrolls are roughly contemporary kinds of Hebrew which are typologically quite different; we have a Hebrew that is close to 'classical' (CD), an apparently living dialect (that of 1QS),[18] and also what is sometimes called 'Tannaitic Hebrew' (4QMMT; the Copper Scroll also contains terms otherwise known only from Tannaitic). The nature of scribally perpetuated languages (such as Latin was in the Middle Ages, or classical Arabic in our own day) is a further factor to be taken into account. It is not uncommon for a scribally transmitted text to preserve archaic forms, even for such a text to be supplemented in its own characteristic language. Scribes whose business it is to copy older texts are quite capable of replicating typologically earlier forms. After all, scribes in Mesopotamia were taught Sumerian, a defunct language, and wrote in it.[19] This does not, of course, mean that scribes

17 I am using the word 'typology' in the sense familiar to archaeologists in classifying pottery, and not as a kind of exegesis familiar in the Church Fathers.

18 See E. Qimron, *The Hebrew of the Dead Sea Scrolls* (HSS, 29), Atlanta: Scholars Press, 1986.

19 A.L. Oppenheim has pointed out (*Letters from Mesopotamia*, Chicago: University of Chicago Press, 1967, p. 20) the phenomenon of a time-lag between the spoken language and the language used for literary purposes in all phases of

could not also sometimes emend texts in a different idiom, confusing the evidence still further.[20] Again, if 'classical Hebrew' were an artificial scribal language, we might find some scribes who were Hebrew speakers writing in a form influenced by oral speech, while others who remained primarily Aramaic speakers would know only the pure form.[21] It is sometimes claimed that scribes of a 'post-classical' period attempting to reproduce 'classical' Hebrew give themselves away by making errors. But such a claim cannot be proven, since if any scribes were successful in avoiding errors, how would we know? And if they knew the language well enough not to make errors, can we say that the language was already dead, or that the scribe was writing in a 'post-classical' age? We care, after all, talking of a relatively brief period from which we have rather little evidence.

Actually, objections to the linguistic arguments do not end here. Underlying the conventional approach to the dating of biblical books by language is the assumption that there is a language called 'biblical Hebrew' examples of which can be dated with reference to its evolution. In a study of this question, E. A. Knauf[22] argues that 'biblical Hebrew' is not a 'linguistic slice' of ancient Hebrew speech. He examines the inscriptional evidence from the Iron Age–Israelite and Judaean–and concludes that on this evidence biblical Hebrew is not (Iron Age) Judaean nor does it correspond to any (sic!) of the Israelite languages, though fragments in such languages might be tentatively identified. Knauf concludes that biblical Hebrew is the language of a literary corpus which arose, in his view, in the exilic and post-exilic period, a *Bildungssprache* whose emergence presupposes the disappearance of the Iron Age Judaean state. On this analysis, 'biblical Hebrew' is another scholarly construct; indeed, we might say that it is

Mesopotamian history. Is this a broader phenomenon?

20   A modern example of the difference between typological and chronological analysis is afforded by the two recently-united German states. The German of former East Germany is, to the ears of West Germans, somewhat archaic.

21   Cf. Oppenheim (*Letters from Mesopotamia*, p. 48) speaks thus of Neo-Babylonian scribes: 'the intelligentsia, on the other hand, also shunned Aramaic words, having created for themselves the image of a direct continuation of the native civilization'.

22   Ernst Axel Knauf, 'War "Biblisch-Hebräisch" eine Sprache?', *ZAH* 3 (1990), pp. 11-23 (who is, of course, borrowing the title from an earlier article [and book title] by E. Ullendorff).

no more than the imputed language of the scholarly 'ancient Israel', and thus part of a larger fabrication.

Because of all these pitfalls, a more nuanced account is needed of the use and character of Hebrew in the Persian-Hellenistic period, in which chronological evolution, dialect development, scribal conservatism, bilingualism, the existence of an artificial literary language and other factors are taken fully into account.[23] It is often said that the inhabitants of Judah spoke Hebrew before the Persian period and Aramaic afterwards. This can hardly be the case. The vast majority of the population, namely the peasants, must have continued speaking the language they spoke for centuries; on the other hand, the immigrants from Babylonia spoke Aramaic. The biblical literature was written in a form of the indigenous language, not the language that the immigrants brought with them, and which no doubt they continued to speak, since it was the *lingua franca* of the western Persian empire. The scribes of Jerusalem were no doubt bilingual (and increasingly trilingual as Greek spread into the Levant); what they spoke at home is hard to guess; what they spoke 'in the office' perhaps depended on whether they were indulging in diplomatic business or librarian duties.

In short, there are *no* linguistic arguments to date the biblical literature to, say, the ninth or seventh century rather than the fifth, and examination of the evidence and arguments for such a procedure does not establish a basis for dating biblical texts but actually exposes the fallacious assumption on which they rest. If there is indeed evidence of linguistic development, I can see no reason why such development is not to be assigned to the period between the sixth and third centuries BCE, during which, I believe, the biblical literature was composed.

---

23   Cf also A. Rofé, 'The Battle of David and Goliath,' in J. Neusner, B. Levine and E. Frerichs (eds), *Judaic Perspectives on Ancient Israel*, Philadelphia: Fortress, 1987, pp. 117-151, p. 125: 'The scribes of the Second Temple period, whose foremost skill was the copying of Scripture, took great pains to transmit their text accurately. In matters of language, for example, they were acquainted with every aspect of classical biblical Hebrew, with its orthography, morphology, lexicon and syntax.....What is true of the scribes is all the more true of the writers who, during the Persian period, at least, attempted to imitate the classical Hebrew of the First Commonwealth.'

## Scribes

The production of literature in Yehud (or any other ancient society) is not a matter of personal initiative nor of the automatic inscribing of whatever oral material is in circulation and in danger of being lost. Writing is an economically supported activity, which requires the specialized knowledge of writing and, not least, a purpose. Reading was not a major leisure activity in the ancient world, though certain groups and individuals did cultivate it. And while it is thus possible that sometimes scrolls were written in order to be read out in liturgical or possibly legal contexts, this explanation does not hold good for most of the biblical literature (Genesis–Kings, Isaiah–Malachi). No: not just what it *is* that is written in the Bible but merely the *fact* that it is written are real and fundamental problems, and largely ignored or brushed aside by most biblical scholars. This literature is neither the product of a total society (95% of it illiterate) nor of isolated individuals but of a class or body, and arises from ideological, economic, and political preconditions.

It is not clear whether in the Persian period there existed two centres of government in Yehud, the temple and the provincial administration. The books of Ezra and Nehemiah are confusing in this respect, and it may well be that the figure of Ezra as a later intrusion reflects a shift in a balance of power between religious and secular authorities. But so long as it can be granted that in Persian period Jerusalem there may have been a provincial administration separate from a temple administration, and so long as it can be allowed that the two centres were probably not in tension, it may be permissible to speak of a single ruling élite, a single administration, and a single scribal class serving a single master. For the purposes of determining the origin of the biblical literature this potential simplification is justified. It is certainly within the orbit of the temple and court that we shall find our authors

For in looking for the origin of literature of any kind, we are looking for a literate class, and in the case of the biblical literature a class which exercises its profession through an institution, namely a scribal school. A scribal school is a *sine qua non* of a developed political and economic system, and in Yehud such a school (or schools) must have existed. The biblical literature is the product of professional writers. Those scholars who appeal to widespread literacy at this time miss the point. The writing of literature such as in the Bible is not a matter having your own seal or being able to scratch your name or even read a simple letter.[24] Even in modern societies with 90% literacy, fewer than 1% write books. At issue is not simply the ability to write, but the capacity, motivation and opportunity to write scrolls and to write *literature*, not to write business transactions, or letters, or lists of names even, or to scratch abecedaries. The production of scrolls containing histories, cultic poems, wise sayings and oracles is not an individual hobby. Such work requires a professional class with time, resources and motivation to write. In some cases it implies access to official archives. These scribes will have been either employed directly by the Temple or court or supported indirectly by them. Many will no doubt have been priests, or perhaps Levites (the name given to those who performed ancillary cultic services but did not belong to the priestly families who came to constitute the ruling class).

These scribes write what their paymasters tell them to, or allow them to, which means generally that they write to safeguard or increase the power and prestige of the monarch or the temple. Their scribal duties cover a wide range of activities, among them the keeping of commercial records (control over the economy), archiving (control and possession of the past, control of the literature class), or history writing (control and possession of the past; matching the claims of neighbouring powers), didactic writing (maintenance of social values among the élite), predictive writing (control over the future).[25]

These scribes not only work for the governing institution; they are also part of it, by being a rather privileged élite. That does not prevent them from criticizing their own régime. There are texts in the Bible that contain quite trenchant denunciation. But this is always expressed in the words of an earlier prophet, so that no direct criticism of the current authorities is explicit. The scribes were in

24   See e.g. A. Millard, 'An Assessment of the Evidence for Writing in Ancient Israel', *Biblical Archaeology Today*, Jerusalem: IES, pp. 301-12. a more extreme and certainly chauvinistic assessment can be found in A. Demsky, 'Writing in Ancient Israel', in M.J. Mulder (ed.), *Miqra* (CRINT II/1), Assen: Van Gorcum, 1988, pp. 2-20.

25   Oppenheim (*Ancient Mesopotamia*, p. 230) classifies the purposes of Mesopotamian writings as follows: administrative recording; codification of laws; formation of a sacred tradition; for annals; for scholarly purposes.

large measure insulated from the majority of the population; physically (they lived in cities), economically (they were supported by the taxpayer) and culturally. How many scribes were there in the society that produced the biblical literature? In the opinion of most modern scholars who have analysed agrarian societies, they will number no more than 5% of the population.[26] The literature of the remaining 95% is oral. The literate and oral segments of ancient society are largely independent of one another. At a royal court, traditional story-telling may furnish a bridge between the two parts of the society; meeting-places such as the city gate, or the market also afford social contact and cultural exchange, and in general we must not rule out contact between popular culture and the world of the scribe. The presence of an artisan and a merchant class affords the opportunity for some social class mobility and a medium for the negotiation of cultural values between the peasants and the governors. But we should never assume, as has often been done by biblical scholars, that popular oral 'traditions' naturally percolate into literature. 'Folk literature' in the Bible is rather more like 'folk music' in the works of Bartok, Janaček or Vaughan Williams.

But an even more intriguing and important question than the authorship of the biblical literature is its readership. The *readers* of this literature, like the writers, must also be *professionally literate*. The literature is not written for the rural agriculturalists, the peasants, for these can neither read, nor, if they could, could afford to obtain scrolls to read, nor if they could do that, would have the time (during daylight hours?) nor, if they had the time, would have the energy or the inclination. The literature is not for a whole society, as supposed by many biblical scholars. It is written largely for self-consumption. The question of why the literature was written, which arises from such an observation, is the subject of the next chapter.

But before turning to that question, let us summarize our profile of the biblical authors (and, as I imagine, readers) in the words of M. Weinfeld:

> persons who had at their command a vast reservoir of literary material, who had developed and were capable of developing a literary technique of their own, those experienced in literary composition, and skilled with the

26   This is a maximal figure, according to J. Baines, 'Literacy and Ancient Egyptian Society', *Man*, London: Royal Anthropological Institute of Great Britain and Ireland, 1983, pp. 572-99, who gives 1% for Egypt 'in most periods'.

pen and the book: these authors must consequently have been the *soferim-hakamim..'*[27]

Weinfeld is talking about the Deuteronomists. In biblical scholarship the scribes are often identified as 'intellectuals'[28] or as 'sages'[29] or as 'the wise,' and especially responsible for 'wisdom literature.' What is perhaps meant is that in this literature one finds an expression of their distinctive outlook on life. But the fact is that *all* of the biblical literature must be a product of this class. What else can we know about them?

We know that they were trained to write in schools. Here their formation into a social class was also reinforced by the inculcation of certain values and perhaps the reading of a sort of 'canonical' repertory, including such works as *Enuma Elish* or *Ahiqar*–or, in due course, perhaps Proverbs or Genesis or Ecclesiastes or Song of Songs. There was in Yehud/Judah, as in ancient Egypt, Babylonia, Assyria, and Persia, Ugarit, Mari, Susa, Damascus, Antioch, a cadre of professional readers and writers, employed to perform tasks which involved studying, classifying, copying and composing. In a study of scribal activity in Mesopotamia, Leo Oppenheim[30] distinguished three particular roles for this class: bureaucrat, poet and scholar. As bureaucrat the sage would be employed by either the palace or the temple (and these were usually closely associated institutions) to keep archives, write annals, compose diplomatic correspondence and liturgical pieces. In ancient Egypt, the scribal schools known as 'houses of life', usually in the proximity of temples, were centres for the 'composition, preservation, study and copying of texts.'[31] The texts were mainly of a religious kind, intended for cultic use, but included magical texts. The term 'academy,' says Williams, 'may be an inaccurate as well as an anachronistic term for it, but it was the resort of the intellectuals of the day'. Its members also composed books of instruction, and attempted to predict the future.

27  M. Weinfeld, *Deuteronomy and the Deuteronomistic School*, Oxford: Clarendon Press, 1972, pp. 177-78.

28  See R.N. Whybray, *The Intellectual Tradition in the Old Testament* (BZAW, 135), Berlin: De Gruyter, 1974.

29  E.g. Gammie and Perdue (eds), *The Sage in Israel and in the Ancient Near East*.

30  L. Oppenheim, 'The Position of the Intellectual in Mesopotamian Society', *Daedalus* 104/2, 1975, pp. 34-46.

31  R.J. Williams, 'The Sage in Egyptian Literature', p. 27.

*Temples*

These scribes were no doubt to be found in centres of administration or of trade. They may even have had residences in villages, and their services may have been available as writers of begging-letters, or even as copiers of prophecies to be sent on to the king or temple. As writers of books, however, they must have worked in a place where the materials for composition were available and where there were incentives for composition. We have a reasonable amount of evidence to associate books with temples or with the royal court. Where literary archives have been unearthed in the ancient Near East they have been either at temple sites, such as at Ugarit, or royal archives, such as at Ebla or Mari or Tell el-Amarna. The royal archive consisted of individual texts, usually storied on shelves and classified.[32] One of the most famous is that of the Assyrian monarch Ashurbanipal, who apparently authorized the copying of ancient texts– an antiquarian enterprise. But there is probably no need to multiply examples; it is well-known that the production and accumulation of literature in the ancient world was associated with palaces and temples, and the archives and libraries which they instituted. Do we, then, have any evidence of such archives or libraries in Yehud? Certainly, the biblical literature itself frequently associates literature with the temple. The 'tables of the law' are described as being stored in the Ark, i.e. in the sanctuary; Joshua's covenant was deposited at Shechem (Josh 24.26); Samuel's 'constitution' of the state is deposited at Mizpeh; Josiah's law-book found in the temple.[33] The biblical literature itself points us firmly enough to its own place of origin. But our comparison should not be confined to the ancient Near East. It is likely that by the end of the fifth century private libraries existed in Greece;[34] according to Strabo (*Geography* 13.1.54) Aristotle had a large collection. So did the Academy, which served as a model for the foundation of the Museum library at Alexandria in the 3rd century

32   For a reconstruction of shelving at Ebla, for example, see G. Pettinato, *The Archives of Ebla*, Garden City: Doubleday, 1981, p.49.

33   These examples I have taken from R.T. Beckwith, 'Formation of the Hebrew Bible', in M.J. Mulder (ed.), *Miqra*, pp. 39-86 (41).

34   The Greek tragedians seem to have used literary sources in their works. Aristophanes pokes fun at Euripides for having used literary sources in composing his tragedies (*Frogs*, 943), but may well have done the same himself.

BCE.[35] In the first century CE Josephus gives us plenty of evidence that the Jewish writings were 'laid up' in the Temple, and rabbinic sources have the same understanding.[36]

It is in the palace or the temple (in our case, the temple) that the written scrolls will have been deposited. We should not rule out the possibility of private copies; a scribe such as Ben Sira may have possessed a limited number of scrolls of his own, perhaps. But in either case these scrolls will have existed for the purposes of the temple–either as an archive, or for temple liturgy, or for recourse in legal disputes, or other economic or diplomatic purposes. We might also consider the Babylonian diviner-scribes who made collections of divination cases which can be traced back to the Old Babylonian period (c. 1900-1600 BCE). These comprised a sort of case-book of interpretation, ostensibly forming a basis for future reference.[37] Omen manuals were certainly in existence by the Neo-Babylonian period (7th–6th centuries BCE).[38] Here, then, we have another instance of texts assembled by diviner-scribes and stored in temple archives. It is also worth noting that this kind of literature was for scribal use: for reference in determining future decisions, or for the education of young scribes in the principles and history of divination. Much the same motivation can be posited for collections of proverbs, psalms and laws. Prophecy is a more interesting case. Among the Mari archives we find not collections of omens, but individual oracle-letters giving, for instance, accounts of dreams which have been sent to the king. Whether these texts were ever studied we cannot be sure. Perhaps they were merely 'filed away'. But at least they were not disposed of. And even such archival work can provide a scribe with sources for literary work. Thus, individual poems can be archived, then subsequently collected into hymnbooks. Individual oracles can be archived, probably under some classification system, and in due course, with proper concern for orderly archiving admixed with creative composition, be collected into scrolls. In saying this, I am supposing that the prophetic books of the Bible may well have a basis in collections of archived materials remaining from the Iron Age.

35   According to Diogenes Laertius 4.1; 5.51.

36   For the references see Beckwith, 'Formation', pp. 42-45.

37   On Babylonian divination, see A.L. Oppenheim, *Ancient Mesopotamia*, pp. 206-27.

38   A.L. Oppenheim, 'A Babylonian Diviner's Manual', *JNES* 33 (1974), pp. 174-220.

What I am certainly not prepared to assume is that these materials existed at this time in the form of scrolls of collected oracles assigned to individual prophets. That *may* in the end be shown to be the case; but *a priori* it seems to me an entirely conjectural supposition, and one which is also unnecessary. The biographical material we have regarding Jeremiah and, to a lesser extent, Isaiah, need not deflect us from realising that in the case of every other prophetic book in the Prophets we have either very little biographicla information, and usually none at all. The figures were unknown to the compilers of the prophetic literature, who knew only the names and probably guessed at virtually everything else.

Among the temples of the ancient Near East, then, we find scribal, schools, archives and libraries. Here are the biblical authors to be found. The next question is *why* and *how* they wrote the kind of literature we find in the Bible. In part we have just seen that materials such as psalms, proverbs and laws are not unexpected. Prophecy is unusual if not unique in the form we have it, though not inexplicable. But there is much else left to be explained.

Chapter Seven

## HOW WAS THE BIBLICAL
## LITERATURE WRITTEN, AND WHY?

There are several phases to be distinguished in the process between the writings we have in the Bible being composed and their being fixed as canonical. As I mentioned earlier, the tendency in much recent biblical scholarship has been to blur rather than to sharpen that sequence of phases by blanketing them in some kind of 'canonical process'. But it has never been satisfactorily explained how or why any body of authors would produce and develop a set of scrolls for the purpose of defining and describing a national religion. This becomes especially problematic if we can find no pre-existent religious system which the literature can define. If the biblical literature is essentially an adventure of creativity, then it is not easy to explain why the authors should wish to invent a set of religious beliefs, a religious system. In whose interest and for what purpose would such an exercise be undertaken? No: what these authors are creating in their literature must be something which their patrons and their profession in some way require them or enable them to do. We have to ask afresh why this literature was created and not start from the knowledge that it later became canonized as scripture. It was not written as a 'Bible', nor even as a set of religious texts.

But between these two ends of the process, the initial composition and the final canonization, there is much to be investigated. Why should it be that these scrolls acquired a religious function and then an extreme religious sanctity? Are we content to accept that somehow it happened, perhaps because the inhabitants of Judah/Yehud/Judaea were especially religious in their disposition? Or should we try to explain the process as precisely as we can, and look for explanations? One aspect of this process is the means by which individual scrolls come to accumulate into series, and then in some kind of archive, so that Josephus, in the first century CE, can say that the Jews/Judaeans have twenty-four books? How did this particular set of scrolls acquire such exclusivity? Hardly because of their religious authority–the question is the other way round–for Josephus they do *not* have a primarily religious quality! The entire process of the formation of this literature and its subsequent fate poses a set of intriguing problems to anyone of an historical bent, and indeed a set of problems which have hardly been formulated, let alone addressed, because the matter has been of no theological relevance or because prevailing assumptions involving 'scripture' obscured the issue.[1]

I shall argue in this and the next two chapters for three stages. The first includes the creation of the 'historical' material, namely from Genesis-Kings, and Chronicles, Ezra, Nehemiah. A second stage is the adoption of the existing historical, and quasi-legal literature as a cultural, then a religious norm for certain groups, in which a kind of exclusive or semi-exclusive piety develops, and with it the addition of some fully religious compositions (Psalms, chiefly) and pious glossing. Finally, there is the official establishment of a set of writings as a national archive, with the cultural and religious authority that impels it on its way towards canonization. These stages are not necessarily in a strictly chronological, nor even typological, sequence, and they constitute only a very rough and preliminary attempt at tackling what is a very large question.

The creation of these scrolls by temple (and/or court) scribes, their retention in an archive, and then their adoption in some official manner as a set of definitive (in some way or other) writings all point to acts dictated by the administration, the ruling class. No such initiative could succeed independently. I have argued in previous chapters that a major motivation of the literary effort of the scribes was the establishment of a national identity in which the status of the existing rulers, of recent immigration, as the indigenous élite, was secured, for their own satisfaction as much as anyone else's. And although the temple cult and the veneration of their own version of

1    In the physical production of scrolls, M. Haran has published a number of articles. See in particular his 'Book-Scrolls in Israel in Pre-Exilic Times', *JJS* 33 (1982), pp. 161-73; 'More Concerning Book-Scrolls in Pre-Exilic Times', *JJS* 35 (1984), pp. 84-85; 'Book-Scrolls at the Beginning of the Second Temple Period: The Transition From Papyrus to Skins', *HUCA* 54 (1983), pp. 111-22. There are also useful essays in H.W. Attridge & J.J. Collins (eds), *Of Scribes and Scrolls*, Lanham: University Press of America, 1990.

the high god (given the name of the local deity, Yahweh, among others) is an element in this endeavour, the endeavour itself is not essentially religious but rather cultural. To describe how one's deity created the universe, gave his adopted people their land, and guided their history does not determine a religion, nor does the historicizing of agricultural festivals betoken a religious tradition. It rather an act of ideological imperialism by which a ruling caste appropriates the native peasant customs and, depriving them of all that is meaningful to the peasant, turns them into celebrations of their own dominant ideology: their acquisition of the law, their deliverance from Egypt, their wandering in the wilderness.

Other parts of the biblical literature are easy to account for: proverbial and cultic collections are widely paralleled in temple archives anyway, and collecting wise words in the name of great king was an idea probably borrowed from Egypt and Babylonia, the two oldest cultures in the ancient Near East. The Psalms are a rather more interesting case. Many of them may indeed be liturgical poetry, written for the temple cult. But a large number betray a personal piety, and their composition needs to be explained accordingly, as I shall attempt in the next chapter. There is evidence that a fixed collection of Psalms came into existence only at the end of the Second Temple period, and the contents may well embrace the whole process of development from the beginnings of the cultural ideology up to the emergence of pious groups for whom the literature was becoming what we would call scripture. The prophetic literature is of even more interest, chiefly because of its curious form. Such highly literary poetry is not what passed for 'prophecy' anywhere else in the ancient Near East, and such parallels as there might be are found in Greece. Where are we to fit the contents of the prophetic books on the trajectory from national history to group piety? Why did the notion of 'prophecy' develop at all? Finally, we ought not to ignore such curiosities as Esther, the Song of Songs, Ruth and Jonah, which belong to a more purely aesthetic category. Yet the inclusion of *purely* aesthetic writings in the biblical corpus is surely also be explained, if that is indeed what they are.

*Ideological preconditions*

What kind of a *ruling caste* needs to produce this sort of literature and preserve it? I have already adumbrated my conclusions in earlier chapters, and here I shall reiterate and develop them. We have in 5th century Yehud/Judah a newly-constructed society without an identity and with a number of tensions (indigenous versus immigrant, homogeneous versus heterogeneous, parochial versus cosmopolitan, urban versus rural, high god cult versus local cults, and many others). We can posit with some probability a conflict between immigrants and indigenous populations, the establishment of a city and temple centre in Jerusalem, the institution of a religious law and bond of allegiance to a deity ('covenant'), and the promotion of an ethnic consciousness as features which constitute the emergence of a governing caste or class. These measures constitute a massive exercise in self-definition, in which I take the creation of the biblical literature to be a further enterprise. The structure of this society has been extensively investigated by Weinberg, Morton Smith, Blenkinsopp and others, using evidence from other contemporary societies. How far the models are reliable depends on how reliable is the picture given in Nehemiah, and I have some doubts about that. But the consensus view sees the immigrants as forming a temple-and Jerusalem-centred exclusive cultic society which controlled in the name of its law the economic and political life of the province, to the initial exclusion of those who could not claim membership by exilic ancestry. The deity worshipped by this society is in character a High God, though he is given the name and some of the titles and peripheral characteristics of a traditional local deity, Yahweh, still widely worshipped in Palestine (and also Transjordan and Syria). But the cult of this god is not the Yahweh cult of Iron Age Palestine: this deity is a single male god, creator of all the earth and all the nations, one who would be recognized elsewhere in the satrapy of Beyond the River as Marduk, or Sin. The Persian monarchs would certainly have no difficulty in recognizing this deity as their lord Ahura Mazda. The adherents of this cult are bound together to exclude non-members. These excluded groups comprise traditional Yahweh worshippers who are acknowledged in Ezra–Nehemiah as being 'people of the land' but who must be shunned. The only place for practice of this cult is the sanctuary and city of this cult-association, Jerusalem, which thus, as the home of the universal Lord of Creation as a very historically important city. In this (quite important) sense there is a central religious dimension to the emerging culture of the ruling caste, namely enthusiasm for a high god cult in a single sanctuary, and a corresponding rejection of other cults. But I would not wish to press the importance of this to the extent of making it the primary factor. It is more, to my mind, a symbol of the cultural superiority of the ruling caste and, of course, a means by which economic exploitation can be practised, since the temple was capable of functioning as an economic tool and not just an ideological one. The establishment of a temple and priesthood, a sacrificial system, a caste system (Weber was not wrong entirely) and an ideology of holiness to support it, were not separable as 'religious' characteristics from other means of political control. To characterize, let alone glorify, these mechanisms as products of religious zeal would be bordering on the ludicrous. The persistent argument of the Former Prophets, that Israel was inherently disobedient and that monarchs precipitated its downfall is a theme perfectly manufactured to justify hierocracy. The categories of 'sin' and 'holiness' are those of the priests; the scribes prefer morality (*ṣedeq, mišpaṭ*), which is a features not just of the so-called 'wisdom' literature but also of the Latter Prophets.

The truth about the society of Yehud is this, then: it is an erstwhile Babylonian province shorn of its ruling class and governed by Babylonians, now become a Persian province and receiving a new population transplanted by the Persians with funds to build a Temple and the city of Jerusalem. This society is constituted by a fundamental contradiction: its élite is aware of its alien origin and culture, but its *raison d'être* implies indigenization: the Persians want the immigrants to accept their new land as their own. So, no doubt, do the immigrants themselves, since it is to be their land. I have raised, and set aside, the question of whether these immigrants were really descended from Judaean deportees. The Persians probably told them that they were, they may have believed it themselves, and it may have been true. But whether or not this were the case, they would have made that claim anyway, and the claim itself is therefore no evidence. (As it happens, the creation of the *bêt 'abôt* shows that some families *needed* fictional genealogical identity.) But in their writings these immigrants set about establishing that claim in no small measure.

This new society generated its own identity, via literature, through the production of a history, in which 'Israel' will function as a key component. This name is chosen to designate the population chosen by Yahweh to inhabit Palestine, bound to it by a law and covenant, and distinguished from other populations by religion and ethnic descent. And since the élite who will generate that history are immigrants, their 'Israel' will also originate as immigrants. The fetish of cultic holiness will serve to strengthen the authority of the priesthood and secure the preeminence of Jerusalem. It will be cultic purity that defines the nation and Jerusalem that assures the deity's presence. Negatively, the 'people of the land' who have *prima facie* a more secure right to the land will be denied that right unless they conform to the cultic and ethnic definition, while those in Samaria, who perhaps continue to use the name Israel, and to worship Yahweh, have to be incorporated into this history, but have also to be ejected from it.

The Pentateuch and the Former Prophets reflect exactly these concerns. We have various stories about arrival in the land, in some cases already equipped with a law, stories about a large empire with Jerusalem and Judah preeminent, a monarchy that built a magnificent Temple, an explanation of why kings led their ancestors into destruction and exile. The Samarians, rivals for political and religious influence in the area and also worshippers of the traditional local deity Yahweh, are cast not only as the enemies of Nehemiah but also as the northern kingdom which seceded from Judah and abandoned Yahweh, while Edomites and Transjordanians, many of whom may also be Yahweh worshippers, are depicted as rejected family members, at least until the Hasmonaeans come along and reverse the policy by making them Judaeans.

I have warned nevertheless against drawing the conclusion that the biblical literature incorporates a seamless ideology. The coherence that there is, which is considerable, is explained by shared preconditions and by a deliberate attempt at some stage to produce a single written history out of a number of alternative and partial ones. The patriarchal stories, the Exodus story and the conquest stories are surely relics of once alternative explanations of land occupation by aliens, later drawn into a single narrative. But the underlying perspective in nearly all these is similar: an alien 'Israel' is given the land by its deity, and occupies it by right, conditional upon scrupulous cultic observance. The poems of Second Isaiah, written in Jerusalem in the 5th century, reveal quite dramatically a process of persuasion to the same end: the immigrants are cast as lost children who have suffered and ought not to be unwelcomed by the indigenous population. The geographical perspective of the writer is clearly from Palestine, though his (her?) sympathies lie with the immigrants. The parallels between these poems and the edict of Cyrus (which Morton Smith saw but which puzzled him because he dated the poems to before the edict) are easily explained if we date the poems later.[2]

The 'exodus', which I have just referred to as one of a number of alternative immigration stories, is currently without any plausible historical basis or other non-historical explanation. There is an overlooked possibility in the Persian period, and rather better than the speculations focussing on the Late Bronze or Iron Age. Since many Judaeans probably went to Egypt at the end of the sixth century and beginning of the fifth, we may expect that some of them returned, whether by free choice or by Egyptian instigation.[3] We know in particular that some Palestinians–Judaeans and Israelites, presumably– had been planted there by the Assyrians as garrison troops, and they write (as the Elephantine letters show) that they are being harassed by the locals. Very possibly, during Egypt's periodic independence from Persia, to whom these Semitic troops were loyal, these garrisons, either voluntarily or under coercion, departed from Egypt and settled in Yehud. (They might even have had a leader with the Egyptian name of Moses!). There is a fourth century Egyptian story (preserved in Hecataeus) that the Jewish priesthood was established by a certain Moses who was an Egyptian and left to found Jerusalem. Is this a garbled version of the exodus story or does it relate the same more recent historical event? At all events, we should not exclude the likelihood of an immigration of people to Palestine from Egypt during this period, and their identification with the dominant culture of Yehud, to which they may have contributed their own claim based

2    M. Smith, 'II Isaiah and the Persians', *JAOS* 83 (1963), pp. 415-20. Cf. also the treatment of Isaiah 40–55 by J.D. Watts, *Isaiah 34-66* (WBC) Waco: Word Books, 1987 and H. Barstad, *A Way in the Wilderness: the 'Second Exodus' in the Message of Second Isaiah*, Manchester: Manchester University Press, 1989.

3    We might also that Ezra 9.1-2 includes 'Egyptians' with Canaanites, Ammonites and Moabites as those from whom the people ought to separate. My suspicion is that these are not native Egyptians (which would be unnecessary) but immigrants from Egypt worshipping Yahweh and claiming to be Judaeans. Jeremiah 44 makes this identification, and opposition to such people, more explicit.

on an escape from Egypt.

The one major argument, of course, which binds the biblical history together is that of continuity: 'Israel' (the true 'Israel') has been in 'Canaan' a long time: the Temple has stood in its site for centuries: the predecessors of the high priests are the kings of Judah (likewise anointed). The ideological triumph of the biblical story is to convince that what is new is actually old. It has been successful to the point of establishing a virtually unchallenged premiss of biblical scholarship. And with this 'Israel' in place, it remains for a entire national culture to be developed. Once the mannequin is assembled, the clothing can be made to fit. Even the non-historical scrolls of the Bible will be linked in a direct or indirect way to the history of the biblical Israel. But it is surely too simplistic to speak in such grand terms of an élite having a history written for it. It cannot be denied that the scrolls, say, of Genesis to Kings are the product of a good deal of rewriting, emending, patching together, sometimes from discrete sources which with some plausibility can be reconstructed. The literature was not produced as a single venture. The implied distinction may be unreal, however. Certainly, the literature was not commissioned and then written to order! But I do think it entirely feasible that the task of constructing a history of the society in which the cult, laws and ethos of the ruling caste would be authorized was undertaken deliberately and conscientiously by the scribes serving the ruling caste, partly at their behest, partly from self-interest, and no doubt partly for sheer creative enjoyment. I do not see why the task needs to have taken more than two or three generations. How it was accomplished exactly we may never know, any more than we can really know whether there ever was a Yahwist or when she or he wrote. But several possible reconstructions might be offered, such as the one that follows.

### *A Model of Scribal Activity*

The following section is an exercise in imagination whose purpose is purely heuristic. It is not to be taken as a hypothesis, since we have too little knowledge of the actual circumstances to test it, and perhaps we always shall. However, it is a valuable discipline for the historian to imagine how any general deductions might imply particular circumstances, institutions and processes. Traditionally, biblical scholars have been reluctant to specify how prophets 'preached' or how psalms functioned in the cult, or the laws of the nation were applied. Sometimes one suspects that biblical historians do not feel they are dealing with a real world at all, but one in which anything might happen. Here, then, is a reconstruction of the way in which the scribal school of the Jerusalem Temple might have produced the scrolls that were eventually to become the Bible. Although only as a suggestion of what *might* have been the case, I think that this kind of analysis may offer a method in which what we can deduce of the composition of the Pentateuch, for example, or the book of Jeremiah, can be explained in terms of actual scribal procedures, and the ideological continuity and discontinuity as well as the widespread cross-referencing and citation between the scrolls can be explained. What follows, I hope, does confirm to what we know of scribal techniques and practices.

The temple school would require the apprentice to learn to write in the scribal language of Hebrew, which was, after all, the ancestral language, though now only spoken by the peasant classes. It comprised five colleges: the college of legal studies, the college of liturgical composition and recitation, the college of sapiential studies, and the college of historiography, and a fifth, which dealt with politics, though of the theoretical kind. (This division does not quite correspond to what Ben Sira says are the studies of a scribe, but it is fairly close). Since college always strive for respectability and antiquity, it is not impossible that they believed themselves to have been founded centuries ago. I prefer the concrete term 'college' to the vaguer but generally preferred 'circle' which typifies the rather vague reference biblical scholarship usually makes to the social context of authorship. If scribes form a 'circle' then they are physically in proximity, and probably institutionally bound. If 'college' seems an unlikely term, then there is also something wrong with 'circle'.

So let us make our model as realistic as we may and consider the colleges. Perhaps the college of liturgical composition came to be named David College, that of sapiential studies Solomon House, and the legal college called the School of Moses. For the historiographical school I cannot imagine a name, though it could fittingly have borne the name of W.F. Albright, since it had a highly optimistic view of what was historical. Of the philosophical college I shall say more presently. Now, the business of scribal schools in the ancient Near East was the preservation, classification, annotation and amplification of the traditional literature. But traditional literature has first to be written: traditions do not materialize out of thin air! There were sources to work on: some individual prophetic oracles, such as were stored at Mari in the form of letters, wisdom sayings, psalms and indigenous legends, perhaps even some scraps of official archives of the kingdom of Judah. These could be, and would be, vastly amplified by borrowing from neighbouring cultures, and by inventing new material of a similar kind. Perhaps the winning scribal student's psalm, appropriately dedicated to the founder of the College, David (or to his Choirmaster), would be added to the archive. The lists of wise sayings, conventionally credited to an ancient figure called Solomon, would grow with every copying.

I imagine the W F Albright institute to have concentrated not only on origins: Abraham, of course, Moses, Joshua, stories of Judges maybe, and a special team will have been set up to work out the chronology of the reigns. Whence the members of this school acquired their data we cannot be sure. It is reasonable to allow that they had access to a list of monarchs who had rules in Israel and Judah, possibly from the records of neighbouring provinces, but quite possibly, too, from native records. There is no reason to doubt that a list of reigns, including one or two incidents, should have been preserved in Jerusalem (then Mizpeh?), and recovered to serve as the basis for the largely fictitious historiographical narratives that were built upon it. But some historiographical material will have arisen from elsewhere too, perhaps. The personalities and biographies of founders of the colleges might have attracted attention. David deserved ample treatment by his own college, who naturally compensated for the limp image of a musician by making him a womanising warrior; likewise the philosophers of the sapiential college dreamed, like their contemporary Plato, of the philosopher-kings, and wrote stories of the great Solomon, turning him into a magnificent emperor, probably against the wishes of the historiographers who, having to explain the separation of the two kingdoms, wanted to find fault with him (and did). They may even have hit back at the college of David by having one of their number compose a court history which showed him as a weak father and monarch. Of Moses, too, to whom was ascribed the origins of the laws from God which first constituted the nation, numerous stories were probably created by the school of legal studies. The political scientists wanted to make him a prophetic figure, since for them the prophet was the ideal statesman. This last proposition needs explaining.

## The Problem of Prophecy

The prophetic material is a particularly interesting case  I have not imagined a school of oracular inspiration. Prophetic oracles are a curiosity, because they are mostly poetry without any context. Most scholars will accept that at least one scroll, Malachi, has created an artificial prophet, and that indeed most 'prophetic' books: certainly Obadiah, Nahum, Habakkuk, cannot be called 'prophetic' in any technical sense. They are actually pseudonymous poetry. Ezekiel is a marvellously literary creation, in which the reader becomes the audience, privy to the prophet's weird inner experiences, but most unlikely to be a record of what anyone ever did. Biblical prophecy has slender roots in any social activity we would call 'prophetic'. Possibly it was informed by contemporary behaviour such as 'street theatre'. But there are difficulties in tracing the materials back to historical figures. Even if we could be confident of the existence of a prophet called Amos who lived in the mid-eighth century BCE, we could not be confident that he was speaking in the name of the god Yahweh, or what his social location was, or what his words were meant to do. For we do not know his society: it is not the biblical 'Israel'. For, from a literal, historical point of view, the words of this Amos are useless for his own time. Prediction of unavoidable doom is not especially useful. The only *point* of such 'prophecies' is as an implied warning to those of a later generation, which leads us to the conclusion that the earliest date for the writing down of the book is several decades after the prophet is supposed to have lived. But what is the *latest* date? That is a question never asked. Now, it is not seriously to be held that Amos, or Hosea had either stenographers or disciples. Equally dubious is the notion that poetic oracles originate in spontaneous prophetic speech. At any rate, the elaboration and collection of such poetic scraps into scroll-length anthologies is a quite separate question from the behaviour of any prophetic individual. The artificiality, the *artifice* of poetic speech itself presents us with a problem about the origin of the 'prophetic' poetry.[4] How much of it may be scribal school exercises, for example? I can think of no reason why large tracts of oracles

4    I am indebted to my colleague David Clines for drawing my attention to this point.

against foreign nations should be carefully preserved over centuries, but I can imagine that if the genre existed, scribes practised it, and how else does one perfect the craft but by composing one's own? And if these are to be preserved, it is useful and necessary to set them in the fictitious past that is burgeoning all around the scribal school. There is *no* necessary, far less automatic, connection between intermediatory behaviour and the production of literature.

What might we make of the social criticism embedded in these texts, the political comment and the ethical teaching?. Aside from the obvious but unlikely one that this literature comes from ancient social protesters who were also spontaneous poets, there are two possible answers, and they are not mutually exclusive. One is that there is no serious purpose, but, as I have suggested, only an effort to master a genre (and improve one's scribal 'classical Hebrew' at the same time. Another is that a good deal of genuine social criticism is embedded here. If so, it would not be surprising to find it in the composition of apprentice scribes, or perhaps even of graduated scribes. Simply because scribes work for the government does not mean that they admire or approve of it. If we have an image of scribes as dull, dusty, pedantic and unimaginative hacks, we, at least as biblical scholars, are condemning ourselves, for they are out forebears. I do not at all resist the idea that there is real anger, real morality, real passion in this poetry. But I see no reason to attribute it to 'prophets' nor to anyone before the fifth century BCE.

Also working against an attempt to historicize the 'prophets' is the complete lack of historical cross referencing within the Latter Prophets. Not only are all but Isaiah (and Jonah) absent from the books of Kings, but they are absent from each other's books. Did Amos have nothing to say about Hosea, or vice-versa? Did Micah never appeal to the example of Isaiah? Did Jeremiah condemn Ezekiel as one of his 'false prophets'? Each of these prophets is unaware, it seems of his contemporaries. The only kind of cross-referencing we *do* get is citation from the words of another prophet, as Mic. 3.12 in Jer. 26.18 (and references to Jeremiah in Ezra 1.1, 2 Chronicles 35 and 36 and Daniel 9. Knowledge, then of other prophets' *words*, but no independent attestation of the historical existence or career of any other prophet. (Just as is thought to be the case with Ezra and Nehemiah). A history of 'prophecy' in 'Israel' is impossible by strict historical methods, for in most cases all one has is a superscription–where even that exists.

We find some evidence of cross-referencing and copying, of course, between Former and Latter Prophets. Portions of 2 Kings duplicate Isaiah and Jeremiah (or vice-versa); Micah and Isaiah overlap a little; the Latter Prophets are frequently dated by the scheme of 2 Kings. But apart from these specific overlaps (and the case of Jonah, a story whose hero appears in 2 Kings), the scribes who were responsible for the prophetic literature worked independently of those composing the historiographical scrolls, who were presumably members of another college. The overlaps are slight and secondary. The same problem arises with the virtual absence of references in the Latter Prophets to the Pentateuchal contents. On a linear 'tradition' model such a lack of cross-referencing has persisted as an unexplained problem. On my model, of scribal colleges working simultaneously in the first instance, and unaware of what was being created elsewhere, or unable to cross-reference what had not yet come into a coherent shape, this problem does not arise.

Finally, on the collegial origin of prophetic literature: I would classify it as broadly political. It deals with social criticism, though always from the aspect of political consequences and implications. Its major prophetic figures are active in political direction or intrigue. It casts its eye beyond its own nation to the deeds of neighbouring states both in the genre of 'oracles against foreign nations' and in its presentation of imperial expansion as punishment for Israel. It also focusses very firmly on the ultimate question of the destiny of history. In fact, if the Latter Prophets have any uniting theme, it is what we call 'eschatology'. Will Israel finally vanquish the other nations (Ezekiel) or will a golden age supervene in which all nations will come to Jerusalem to worship Yahweh (Isaiah)? Are the other nations on a par with us so as to be punished like us (Amos), or so as to be forgiven (Jonah)? Hence the name I suggest for the fifth scribal college is the school of politics. Perhaps this college also became interested in manticism and produced apocalypses–but this is a largely non-biblical matter and not to be raised here.

### *'Law'*

The school of legal studies was not a legislative body. The nature and status of 'law' in the Bible (and in 'ancient Israel') has been gradually transformed in recent years by the realization that the so-called biblical lawcodes are not descriptions of how law was actually imposed.[5] Law was probably for the most part traditional, enforced by village or in city gate, and to whatever extent the king wished, by himself. The study of Deuteronomy by M. Weinfeld[6] was influential in establishing that its writers were scribal theorists. More recently, E. Otto has argued that the 'Book of the Covenant' and the Code of Eshnunna are each lists of exemplary cases from which legal principles might be explored and developed by scribes, and not necessarily to be directly enforced.[7]

Nevertheless, many scholars still suppose that what Ezra brought to the people of Jerusalem and had read out in Neh. 8, the 'book of the law of Moses' was either the Pentateuch, or Deuteronomy, or the Priestly Code, or some part of what is now in the biblical literature. There are two problems with this, one being that the story of Ezra may well be quite unhistorical. We can at best ask of this very suspect account, 'what is it that Ezra is *presented* with having brought? And the answer is: a written book of laws ascribed to Moses, almost certainly meant to be whatever the 'law of Moses' implied when this story was written. I take the story in fact to be very late (Ezra is unknown to second century BCE Jewish writers) and to reflect a situation in which five scrolls, or perhaps the one scroll we call Deuteronomy, were taken to be a legal basis for proper Judaean/Jewish conduct.

It is nevertheless reasonable to think that the Persians encouraged the development of a local Judaean law, as was their policy elsewhere in their empire, so that a process of codification (or creation) of laws, by a scribal college, is likely. However, I doubt that we can distil from what we know have in the literature what that original code might have been. The biblical 'laws' are the result of a good deal of

5    For a clear account of the position, see Rogerson, in J.W. Rogerson and P.R. Davies, *The Old Testament World*, Cambridge: CUP, 1989, pp. 233-52.

6    M. Weinfeld, *Deuteronomy and the Deuteronomistic School*, Oxford: Clarendon Press, 1972.

7    E. Otto, *Rechtsgeschichte der Redaktion im Kodex Ešnunna und in 'Bundesbuch'* (OBO, 85), Freiburg: Universitätsverlag, 1989.

scribal elaboration, mostly theoretical. Accordingly, it is incautious to assume that the legal parts of the biblical literature are necessarily the oldest. The most developed are the cultic regulations, in which temple practices (partly inherited, partly innovated) are extended into a theoretical picture of a twelve-tribe Israel in a camp with a tent, which itself presupposes a good deal of development of the historiography. 'Torah' as meaning a written set of laws, as a scripture, is by no means necessarily a relatively early development. One can see this development taking place in certain Psalms and to have gone a long way in Ben Sira. But while the creation of legal 'traditions' is undoubtedly an important part of the overall scribal activity in the Second Temple, the view that biblical law forms the foundation for both the rest of the biblical literature and the development of Judaean culture ('Judaism') needs reassessing. The evidence of the Mishnah itself suggests rather differently; its structure and content both imply that there was no established place for the biblical laws in the conduct of Judaean society, as opposed to the practices of certain groups who in any case concentrated their attention on purity laws and not civil behaviour.

The college of legal studies, then, is concerned with elaborating a theoretical definition of 'Israel', a 'legal culture' and not–apart from the important exception of cultic regulations–consciously laying the foundation for the practical conduct of members of the society.

### *Priestly versus scribal interest?*

It is noteworthy that there is little overlap between the 'prophetic' and the 'historiographic' literature, nor any within the individual books. I noted earlier that whereas the Former Prophets (historiography) and indeed perhaps Genesis-Kings on the whole tend to reflect an ethos of holiness, cultic regularity, legal requirement, the Latter Prophets display an interest in justice and morality which scholars frequently identify with 'wisdom'. This distinction should not be pressed too far, for there are numerous exceptions. But it does prompt us to recognize two different sub-cultures here, one being priestly and the other, for want of a better characterization, the scribal. I shall use this shorthand despite the fact that the 'scribal' is not necessarily non-priestly, nor was the priestly view held by all priests or only by priests. Might this be accounted for by suggesting that certain of the scribal colleges were dominated by priestly scribes or priestly patrons, while others were not? The covert or overt criticisms of obedience to cult and law, even to priests, which are found especially in the Latter Prophets, just as these issues are largely ignored in the wisdom books offer scope for a broader *ideological analysis* which might aid in locating different interests within the scribal profession. The argument can be pushed a little further by concentrating on key figures. While there are signs of Moses being profiled as both priest and prophet (I take the prophet to be a scribal and not a priestly character), Enoch is a wisdom figure, while in Nehemiah and Ezra we may have the candidates from either side offered in competition for the role of founders of Judaism, as argued by Kraemer.[8] According to this line of argument, the two subcultures struggled and were partly reconciled, with the priestly perspective largely winning, as its own definition of Torah as written law prevailed over a broader scribal definition, with the creation of the very priestly prophet Ezekiel, with the glossing in Chronicles of the prophet as levite, even in Deuteronomy with the speech before battle delivered by a priest. Ben Sira, who venerates Enoch and ignores Ezra (whom he has perhaps never heard of), nevertheless adores the high priest but does not yet accept that 'torah'=written law. It is, I think, possible that a struggle between priestly and non-priestly elements in Second Temple society might be seen within the literature, though it is always hazardous to assign such ideological differences to well-defined groups. This ought to be resisted in favour of a model which seeks merely to determine the extent of influence of each ideology on the authorship(s) of particular biblical scrolls. Whether the scrolls of torah and the scrolls of prophecy in the way that Blenkinsopp does,[9] with the latter as a corrective to the former, I doubt, so long as the relationship is seen as chronological; as representing an ongoing tension between different ideologies, this view is clearly and attractively put.

Of course this model explains only the possible origin of certain complexes of material. Whether these complexes would have been

8    This interesting argument is put forward by D. Kraemer in a forthcoming article in *JSOT*, 'On the Relationship of the Books of Ezra and Nehemiah'. Further implications about the historicity or non-historicity, and the ideological programme of the Ezra-Nehemiah narratives are contained in T.C. Eskenazi, *In an Age of Prose. A Literary Approach to Ezra–Nehemiah* (SBLMS, 36), Atlanta: Scholars Press, 1988.

9    J. Blenkinsopp, *Prophecy and Canon. A Contribution to the Study of Jewish Origins*, Notre Dame, University of Notre Dame Press, 1977.

interweaved within my posited individual schools is hard to say. It should be remembered, however, that on my model many scribes graduated from more than one school so that any composer of a prophetic story would know how a messenger-oracle was to be formulated. I imagine scribes to have moved between colleges or for material to have passed between colleges. It is also taken for granted that the best scribes were able to write if necessary in many styles, especially 'Deuteronomistic' prose. The phenomenon of inner-biblical exegesis is nicely explained on the basis of a scribe carrying over from one piece of work to another, or from his reading to his writing desk, a phrase or an idea. I would certainly prefer a synchronic rather than a diachronic account of this process, and for that reason doubt the philosophical, perhaps sophistic distinction made by Fishbane between *traditio* and *traditum*. Fishbane's study is an excellent piece of taxonomy, flawed only by what I think is an entirely wrong, though widely shared, matrix of interpretation.[10]

On the other hand, there are curious *lacks* of overlap. As Rendtorff has pointed out, references to the Pentateuchal material are unknown in what he calls the 'pre-exilic' literature,[11] there is disagreement about whether there are documentary sources,[12] and if so, when they are to be dated. But the problem is not merely 'pre-exilic': are the contents of the Pentateuch known to the Chronicler and the writers of Ezekiel? Since Chronicles also elevates David at the expense of Moses, might we assign its authorship to a revision of a draft which another college turned into the scrolls of Kings? Do we *have* to suppose a theological bias rather than ignorance on his part? Given what must have been a very restricted circle of scribes, it is very hard to explain the problem Rendtorff identifies, while failure to establish a secure chronological sequence for the presumed 'sources' is a serious shortcoming. The model I am suggesting, and indeed the thesis of the whole book, though only minimally developed and not without its own

10   M. Fishbane, *Biblical Interpretation in Ancient Israel*, Oxford: Clarendon Press, 1985.

11   R. Rendtorff, *The Problem of the Process of Transmission of the Pentateuch* (JSOTS, 89), Sheffield: JSOT Press, 1990 (German 1977).

12   Cf. for a critique, R.N. Whybray, *The Making of the Pentateuch: A Methodological Study* (JSOTS, 53), Sheffield: JSOT Press, 1989; for an alternative proposal, Rendtorff, *The Problem of the Process*, and T.L. Thompson, *The Origin Tradition of Ancient Israel: The Literary Formation of Genesis and Exodus 1–23* (JSOTS, 55), Sheffield: JSOT Press, 1989.

problems to address, provides an alternative context in which the whole issue might be reconceived. A diachronic analysis, relying upon 'traditions' stretching over several centuries, is historically baseless, creates more problems than it solves, and, of course, requires the existence of 'ancient Israel'. The development of 'tradition' over a matter of a few generations, and more or less simultaneously, is a model to which I hope scholars will devote as much attention in future.

### Function of the end-product

What is the practical outcome of the production of these schools? Apart from the scholarly and aesthetic, there needs to be a political application, since the scribal school is an instrument of state. The result is a literary objectification of the state (by which I mean its rulers), by means of a widely-defined cultural repertory, including a history, a wisdom 'tradition', a cultic repertory and other kinds of literature which any such state should have in order to gain credibility and respectability, and which we know at least Egypt and Babylon, possibly some Phoenician cities, to have possessed. The achievement is not merely intellectual but political in the sense that with its completion, something has been defined that can be called 'Judaean'. With the biblical literature emerges the possibility of 'Judaism' in the cultural sense, and, very importantly, *in an exportable sense.* Whoever reads this can appreciate what being Judaean (whether Judaean in Babylon, Damascus, Alexandria, Tyre, or Antioch) means. All those affiliated to Yahweh, resident in Palestine, or wishing to adhere to either, can claim a cultural heritage of some magnificence. Not, I stress, at this stage, a religion. Anyone (like Jonah) who wants to say 'I am a Judaean/Jew, worshipper of Yahweh' can know what kinds of behaviour, attitude and belief might be appropriate to that claim. In the same way, the historiographical writings of Manetho, Berossus, and perhaps Philo of Byblus, which embrace the origins of the race from Creation until the present or the recent past, are examples of literature produced by other societies for similar reasons. In particular, the sequence of scrolls from Genesis to Kings is the result of an editing of their contents in such a way as to provide an unbroken continuous account of the origins of 'Israel' to the point at which the origins of the society *really* begin.

But all this came about only by a certain amalgamation and juxtaposition of discrete compositions. We have to posit a process in which a continuous large-scale history emerges from a sequence of scrolls, no doubt preceded and accompanied by discussion and evaluation of the materials newly made available for such arrangement. The individual character of the biblical scrolls (or books as they are now known) is rather more impressive than their consistency, and it seems to me more plausible to conclude that they were made to conform to one another at a secondary stage rather than result from the arbitrary breaking of a larger composition into scroll-length sections. Hence although I am determined to consider Genesis-Kings as a single literary work, this is only by virtue of its scrolls having been copied and recopied, and shelved, in such a way that they could be read continuously to give a single narrative. Accordingly, I doubt whether the term 'Deuteronomistic History' should continue to be used by scholars as if it were a fact instead of a theory.

A continuous process, then, of cross-referencing, harmonising, chronological adjustment and explanatory glossing will have ensued as soon as the various pieces of literature assumed a shape. All this can be seen as a process of organic growth and exactly as a scribal school would be expected to perform. The distinction scholarship has imported between text and interpretation, scripture and midrash is false, for the task of rewriting is at the same time a task of organizing, rationalizing and other forms of emendation. It is *this* process which most closely approximates to what scholars call 'tradition', though it can more concretely be designated as the normal practice of scribal treatment of literature. From an analysis of features in the Greek translation of the literature, Gooding has arrived at the following description of scribal activity which is not far from what I am proposing for the organic process by which the literature grows into the shape it finally presents:[13]

> To account for the present state of the text seems to require something more like a rabbinic school, a Beth hamidrash, where varying Hebrew text-traditions and the comparative merits of alternative Greek renderings could be discussed; where opposite verdicts on the characters of the leading figures in the Book–David, Solomon, Jeroboam, Ahab–could be debated; and where in the light of the prevailing views the Greek

13   D.W. Gooding, *Relics of Ancient Exegesis. A Study of the Miscellanies in 3 Reigns 2*, Cambridge, CUP, 1976, pp. 111-2.

translation could, where necessary, be worked over and revised; where apparent contradictions.....could have different solutions applied to them.....

A major part of the process of fitting together stories of creation, of the nation's ancestor, of laws, of acquisition of the land, of loss of the land involved determining in which sequence various origin stories might be assembled–for instance, that Moses ought to come before Joshua but after Joseph and the judges-stories before Saul but after Moses. The process is very similar to that described by Noth in his *History of Pentateuchal Traditions*, where what he calls 'themes' were integrated. Rather than envisage large-scale conceptions at the outset, we might better imagine a process of editing in which the various scrolls were shelved in what was decided was a chronological sequence. In the process of copying, the gaps between the scrolls would then be filled. In this stage, which might be called a large-scale editing, we might see the incorporation of Deuteronomy in its present place, the wedging of Judges between Joshua and Saul, and the distribution of the legal material into the historiographical narrative. The existence of legal materials within segments of historiographical ('ethnographical' might be better) is perhaps best explained either by the overriding need of an historiographical framework, or, as is in my view more probable, the belief that these legal materials ought to have an ancient setting, and that since they comprise the 'constitution' of the nation, quite properly belong in the account of its origins. My purpose, however, in these observations, is to point to signs of large-scale organization of the materials, a process which cannot plausibly be confused with its composition. In other words, the production of a large-scale and complete history from the creation to the beginning of the society of Yehud was not the primary task. That goal was subsequently achieved by the production of partial accounts, sometimes contradictory accounts. Such a procedure is entirely explicable, for no overall blueprint of the history to be written was drawn up in advance. There *was* no pre-existent history to be written about, no 'tradition', and so various accounts had at first to be invented, and only at a secondary stage were they reconciled and combined into a fairly coherent sequence of scrolls. This is not a trivial point. That there was no 'national tradition' to begin with is extremely important to understand. Such an absence follows from what I have said about the non-existence of 'ancient Israel' and explains many of the features of the biblical historiographical narrative that resulted.

### From writing to reading and critique

Thus, by sometime in the third century we have a substantial national archive, though how fixed or 'official' we cannot yet say, housed within the scribal schools, presumably within the temple complex. Furthermore, two tendencies can be noted within the continuing development of the scrolls. First, an inclination on the part of some groups and individuals to use these writings as a definition of what it is to be a Judaean. This was, as I said earlier, a primary outcome, though only an implicit purpose, of the enterprise, and there is no reason why sons should not take what their fathers write as being the truth, if one can really put it so bluntly. It is, after all, a biblical ethic. It is well known by students of such things that traditions come and go very quickly and need no more than a generation to become established. In the United Kingdom the celebration of Christmas and the Scottish 'highland culture' are only two of a large number of 'traditions' less than two centuries old.

But not all scribes were so deferential to their own artistic products. A second tendency is found among some, like the writers of Job, Ecclesiastes, Jonah, and those who wrote up stories about David and Solomon, who were less reverential and attacked the hagiographic tendencies of the literature. They satirized, for instance, the simplistic retributional theory which had become the official college line (we call it Deuteronomistic). Their writings, however, also become incorporated into the collection of scrolls, as did the criticisms of the prophetic writings to which I referred earlier and the pious compositions found among the Psalms. This again is a well-known phenomenon: the fate of the best critics of an establishment is to be included posthumously within it, since their criticism is more damaging outside it. At all events, the literary adventure continued well into the Hellenistic period. The biblical literature (as, we must remember, it was to *become*) was not a closed corpus, nor were its views sacrosanct–at least, not to everyone. There is as yet no such thing as we might call 'scripture'. That, as the next chapter argues, is on the way, and only gradually.

Chapter Eight

## FROM LITERATURE TO SCRIPTURE

*In what sense can we speak of 'Scripture'?*

In the previous chapter I traced the emergence of the biblical literature to national ideological factors, a need to define a society and create a culture on the part of a ruling caste and the scribes who served them. The subject matter of this chapter is the transition from the production of the literature, by which I mean both its inception and its continual growth, to its achievement of a more or less finished form and its adoption by certain individuals and groups as the basis of a national culture. A particular instance of this adoption, and one which forms the core of this chapter, is the veneration, also by certain groups and individuals, of these scrolls as a religious text, as an object of pious and not just educative study.

Despite the title of the chapter, it is important to realize immediately that there is no way of distinguishing in Hebrew, Aramaic or Greek between 'scripture' and 'literature', and so the modern distinction, if it is valid, needs to be spelled out in other terms.[1] Indeed, the distinction, even if proper, may nonetheless be as much a liability as an asset, since where a major element of cultural identity is religious, a national literary heritage will function in ways which might strike us a 'scriptural'. But we can, or should, recognize the difference between quasi-religious reverence and religious devotion. The works of Homer were subjected to textual scrutiny, emendation and comment. They were the basis of a good Greek education, they were subject to commentary. Does this make them *scriptural*? It may be beneficial, if we nevertheless want to speak of Jewish 'scriptures' to remind ourselves of the terms in which Jews of the late Second Temple period (and even a little later) referred to what *we* call their 'scriptures'. When Jews spoke in Greek, for

1    Also pointed out by J. Barr, *Holy Scripture: Canon, Authority, Criticism*, London: SCM, 1983. p. 50.

example, of *graphē* they might have meant 'scriptures', but if they wanted to make it clear that they wanted to distinguish these from non-scriptural literature, they could, and did, speak of *hosiai graphai,* 'holy literature' (Rom. 1.2). Thus 2 Peter 3.16 seems to refer to the writings of Paul and other *graphē* (most English translations give 'scripture' here), while Matthew 26.56 has *graphē t ōn prophētōn,* better translated 'writings of the prophets' or 'literature of the prophets' than 'scriptures of the prophets'. In Philo and Josephus we find *hai graphai* and also *ta hiera grammata*.[2] The rabbinic literature speaks of 'scrolls[3] that defile the hands' and 'scrolls that do not', terminology suggesting again that while there is a distinction here, our own criteria regarding 'literature' and 'scripture' may not be appropriate. The same is true of the Hebrew terms *hmqra*, 'what is read' and *hktwb*, 'what is written', since *hktwbym* means '*the* literature', i.e. specific writings, and *hsprym* 'the (specific) scrolls'. 4 Ezra (late 1st century CE) tells a story of Ezra's reconstitution of the lost scrolls of the Jews. He dictated ninety-four books (actually 'tablets'), of which twenty four were to be made public and seventy reserved for the 'wise among your people' (14.19-48). It is interesting that although we have here the total number of books corresponding to those in the Hebrew Bible, they are if anything of less value than the non-Biblical books! Of particular concern is the way in which the contents of these twenty-four books are described. Ezra says (14.21-2):

> 'Your law has been burned, and therefore no-one knows the deeds that have been done and are to be done by you. If then I have found favour with you, send the Holy Spirit to me and I shall write down all that has happened in the world from the beginning, the things which were written in your law, that humans may be able to find the way and those who wish to live in the last days may live'

It seems, if we have the text correctly transmitted, that the twenty-four books are all referred as 'the law', but also described as being books of *historical* content. Cf also John 10.34 which refers to Psalm 82 as law. The Psalms are also cited as 'law' in Rom. 3.19 and Isaiah in 1Cor 14.21.

2  For a fuller list, see Beckwith, 'Formation', pp. 39-40.
3  'Scrolls' is more accurate than 'books,' although the word *megillah* is more strictly 'scroll' than *sepher*. But the physical nature of writing is an important dimension of this investigation, and it is better to be pedantic than misleading.

In Josephus (*Against Apion* 1.37-43) the picture is only slightly different:

> It therefore naturally, or rather necessarily follows (seeing that with us it is not open to everybody to write the records, and that there is no discrepancy in what is written; seeing that, on the contrary, the prophets alone had this privilege, obtaining their knowledge of the most remote and ancient history through the inspiration which they owed to God, and committing to writing a clear account of the events of their own time just as they occurred)–it follows, I say, that we do not possess myriads of inconsistent books conflicting with one another. Our books, those which are justly accredited (*ta dikaiōs pepisteumena*) are but twenty-two and contain the record of all time. Of these, five are the books of Moses, comprising the laws and the traditional history down to the death of the lawgiver.....From the death of Moses until Artaxerxes who succeeded Xerxes as king of Persia, the prophets subsequent to Moses wrote the history of the events of their own times in thirteen books. The remaining four books contain hymns to God and precepts. From Artaxerxes to our own time the complete history has been written, but has not been deemed worth of equal credit with the earlier records because of the failure of the exact succession of the prophets.
>
> We have given practical proof of our reverence for our own writings. For, although such long ages have now passed, no one has ventured either to add, or to remove, or to alter a syllable; and it is an instinct with every Jew, from the day of his birth,to regard them as the decrees of God, to abide by them, and, if need be, to die cheerfully for them. Time and again ere now the sight has been witnessed of prisoners enduring tortures and death in every form in the theatres, rather than utter a single word against the laws and the allied documents (*tas meta toutōn anagraphas*).

Josephus claims that the Jews have twenty-two books, writings which are regarded as 'decrees of God'. There are, he admits, other books, but these are not 'justly accredited' since they were not written under inspiration, which means they were not written by prophets–a prophet being, I think, someone who writes (or speaks) under divine inspiration. It is not clear that Josephus is making a threefold distinction between law, prophets and other writings, as is often claimed. It seems to me more likely that even Moses is presented as a prophet, while the books of 'hymns to God and precepts for the conduct of human life' are also prophetic.[4]

We should note from this passage two things: first, that Josephus

4    This is suggested by J. Barton, *Oracles of God. Perceptions of Ancient Prophecy After the Exile*, London: Darton, Longman and Todd, 1986, pp. 40-41 and p. 49 n. 32.

*does* distinguish between is law and 'allied writings', and second, that he seems to regard as of the highest importance the matter of historical veracity. Regarding the law as 'decrees of God' needs little explanation–but why the prophets? Josephus seems to be saying that they are venerated as such because they are inspired historical writing. This view, then, of the Jews' books is not so very different from 4 Ezra. It agrees at least on seeing these books as *history*, although this history includes laws.

A division of the 'books' into two classes rather than three (as in the Masoretic Bible) is easier to sustain than a division into three. Barr had already decided that by 'prophets' was meant 'non-Torah materials'[5] and Barton has more recently argued quite convincingly for seeing the term 'prophets' as embracing a loosely-defined collection of non-Torah scrolls. Thus, in the Gospels, with the single exception of Luke 24.44, which adds 'the psalms', we find the phrase 'law and prophets' regularly used for what we moderns term 'the scriptures'. These were not necessarily seen as a bound pair, either: the Samaritans held the law separate, and works such as 4 Maccabees also refer only to the law. Philo, too, wrote only in interpretation of the books of the law, and half of his very few non-Pentateuchal references are from Psalms and Proverbs.[6] Of interest, however, is his regular description of statements from the law of Moses as 'oracle' (*chrēsmos*) or 'logion'. Moses is thus presented as in much the same way as prophets; Jeremiah as much as Moses is designated 'hierophant'. Philo's usual designation is 'holy books', 'holy oracles' 'holy writings'. In the *Letter of Aristeas*, also from Alexandria, some 200 years earlier, the terminology is similar: 'holy law' and 'oracles'.

Among the Dead Sea Scrolls[7] we appear to have evidence of the existence of all the biblical scrolls except Esther, although this statement requires reservation until all the materials have been published. It has not proved possible to decide whether any dividing line exists in this literature between what we call 'scriptural' and other books. For example, in CD 4.15 the phrase '*šr* '*mr*, used to introduce

5    Barr, *Holy Scripture*, p. 55.

6    For a convenient review of Philo's use of earlier writings, see Y. Amir, 'Authority and Interpretation of Scripture in the Writings of Philo', *Miqra*, pp. 421-53.

7    See J. Fitzmyer, 'The Use of Explicit Old Testament Quotations in Qumran Literature and in the New Testament', *NTS* 7 (1960-61), pp. 297-333; M. Fishbane, 'Use, Authority and Interpretation of Mikra at Qumran', *Miqra*, pp. 339-377.

citations from books now in the Bible, precedes a citation from 'Levi son of Jacob.' The formulas for citation consist of either *ktwb* or *'mr*, sometimes followed by the name of the writing and sometimes not. It is of course quite clear that such citations are from authoritative books, but what terms do we find to designate something corresponding to our 'scripture'? The clearest evidence occurs in 1QS 1.3, 'as he [God] commanded by the hand of Moses and all His servants the prophets'. A similar conjunction of Moses and the prophets occurs in 1QS 8.15-16 and in CD 5.21-6.1, while the phrase 'law of Moses' occurs in 1QS 5.8 and 8.22; CD 15.2,9.12 etc. In CD 7.17 occurs 'the books of the prophets'. Putting aside, then, the question of how these were regarded, we can conclude from this evidence that the law of Moses and 'books of prophets' were regarded as authoritative in some way, though we cannot be certain whether there was any defined list of contents of the latter. In 11QPs$^a$ 27, a catalogue of David's poetry concludes with the words 'all these he spoke through prophecy which was given to him from before the Most High.'

In 1 and 2 Maccabees the evidence is less straightforward. 2 Macc 15.19 also has 'law and prophets'. But we find somewhat less certainty in the matter of designation: 2.13 refers to 'the records' and 'the memoirs of Nehemiah' and reports that Nehemiah founded a library and 'collected the scrolls about the kings and the prophets, and the writings of David, and letters of kings about votive offerings.' Here it is not at all clear which of the literature referred to is now in the Bible and which not. 2 Macc 8.23 describes how Eleazar read aloud from 'the holy book' (singular) before a battle. Although there is no way of telling which book this might have been, it is Deuteronomy among the biblical books that describes the speech of the priest before battle, and I suspect that this the 'holy book' referred to.

Thus, in the first century BCE it does not seem that the term *graphē* or any Hebrew equivalent, was used to designate what we call 'scripture': 1 Macc 12.21 reads 'it has been found in *graphē* concerning the Spartans and the Jews', clearly not meaning any biblical literature. Rather, we meet the term (1 Macc 12.9) 'the holy books that are in our hands.' In 1.56 is the following: 'the books of the law which they found they tore to pieces and burned with fire. Where the book of the covenant was found in the possession of anyone, or if anyone adhered to the law, the decree of the king condemned him to death'. Here, as in 2 Macc 8.23, I think that what we know as the book of Deuteronomy is singled out ('book of the covenant).

We end this brief survey in the 2nd century BCE. In the prologue to the translation of Ben Sira's writings, his grandson speaks of 'the law and the prophets and the others that followed them...the law and the prophets and the other books of our fathers...the law itself, the prophecies and the rest of the books'. Again, while it is tempting to deduce from this a three-fold emerging 'canon', we should note that no distinction seems to be made between these books and the writing whose translation Ben Sira's grandson is recommending to his readers. In other words, the wisdom of Ben Sira is in the line of the earlier writings too. This continuity between the writings of the past and more recent writings is suggested even in the famous description of the scribe by Ben Sira himself (39.1-3, 6-8):

> .....he who devotes himself
> to the study of the law of the Most High
> will seek out the wisdom of all the ancients
> and will be concerned with prophecies;
> he will preserve the discourse of notable men
> and penetrate the subtleties of parables;
> he will seek our the hidden meanings of proverbs
> and be at home with the obscurities of parables...
> If the great Lord is willing
> he will be filled with the spirit of understanding
> he will pour forth words of wisdom
> and give thanks to the Lord in prayer.
> He will direct his counsel and knowledge aright,
> and meditate on his secrets.
> He will reveal instruction in his teaching
> and will glory in the law of the Lord's covenant.

So far, this rather lengthy review has taken us backwards to the beginning of the second century BCE and shown that there is no evidence of a consistent and clear understanding of what 'scripture' might contain or mean. But can we fix a point at which this literature, however understood, achieved a fixed form?

According to our witness, a late 3rd century BCE scribe, Ben Sira, the wise man, the scribe, studies all sorts of literature, and adds to it; law, prophecies and proverbs are the kinds of writing he refers to. It might be suspected that in opening with 'law' and 'prophecies' Ben

Sira is betraying the existence of specific categories attested later. But let us remind ourselves that in Daniel 9, which is probably written not a great deal later, Daniel finds a prophecy of Jeremiah 'in the scrolls'. It is not clear that at the beginning of the 2nd century BCE we have a set of authoritative writings clearly separated from others, nor a clear distinction between writing them and studying them. The process of writing 'scripture' has not come to an end, and whether there is in any sense a fixed corpus (even if capable of being extended) remains to be discovered, as does the mechanism by which such a 'fixing' could in fact take place.

But there may more to be said about the fixity of the biblical literature at the beginning of the second century BCE. The collections of Greek translations do not suggest a restricted number of books, nor an agreed sequence, other than that dictated by logic. As far as the textual forms are concerned, of course, we know that there was fluidity in both 'law' and 'prophets'. And at the point when the Old Greek translation of Jeremiah was made, there existed at least two quite discrepant versions of the book of Jeremiah. But what about the content of even the 'law'? Here is some evidence that the 'law' during this period was not necessarily in the form of the five books of Moses that our bibles now contain. The evidence is not much, but then neither is it the other way. I begin with the distinction between the 'books of the law' and the 'book of the covenant' in 1 Macc 1.56, and the reference to the 'holy book' in 2 Macc 8.23, which I suggested was also Deuteronomy. Finally, in Ben Sira 24.23 is a reference to the 'scroll of the covenant of the Most High God, the law which Moses commanded us...' Can this really be a reference to *five* scrolls of law? Or is it, with its reference to 'covenant', the book we know as Deuteronomy, or a form of it? It is, after all, generally accepted by scholars that the book of Deuteronomy forms a distinct and detachable element within the Pentateuch, and the only question I am raising is when, and perhaps how gradually, the position of Deuteronomy was firmly fixed after the scroll of Numbers and its ending adjusted accordingly. I shall argue presently that the independence of Deuteronomy is also attested in the books of Ezra and Nehemiah (whenever they are to be dated). The strong influence of Deuteronomy in the Temple Scroll is also noteworthy, and it may be worth asking whether for its author this book was considered separate from the other books of what became known as 'torah', and the purpose of the Temple Scroll, perhaps among other things, was to reconcile them.[8]

As for the remainder of the 'law', or the 'pentateuchal' tradition, and what we call the 'Former Prophets' there is also some evidence that these were not quite fixed in their present shape in the time of Ben Sira. In chapters 44–50, the eulogy of 'famous men' of the past, this old scribe shows acquaintance with the contents of Genesis–Kings and Nehemiah (not Ezra), which he follows, with some deviations. He begins with Enoch, omits any reference to Joseph or the Exodus or to Joseph, but then returns to Enoch again at the end followed by, most curiously, Joseph, Shem, Seth and Adam, 'above every living being in the creation'. It is, of course, always possible to explain away such divergences from the biblical sequence. But 'explaining away' is not the point of criticism. Rather, here is a question mark: were stories about Adam and Enoch, for example, truncated later than the time of Ben Sira? The evidence of the Masoretic text itself certainly suggests that certain material has been deliberately omitted. The account of Enoch in Gen. 5.21-24 suggests a remarkable figure but says nothing more than that he 'walked with God and was not, for God took him'. The importance of Enoch for Ben Sira (Enoch is after all the only one mentioned twice, and he starts off the parade) is hardly explained by the biblical data alone. Ben Sira knew more about Enoch. But did his knowledge come from other literature? Did he make no distinction in his eulogy between the record now preserved in the Bible and non-biblical ones? It is possible, but by no means to be taken for granted, especially in view of Ben Sira's generally close adherence to the 'biblical' narrative.

There is some supporting evidence for the view that the Genesis story in what became the Masoretic form of the Hebrew text was still being developed at this period. There is a fairly obviously truncated text in Genesis 6.1-4, containing an allusion which makes sense only when the story of the fall of the Watchers, told in Enoch 6-11 and Jubilees 5.1-11, is taken into account.[9] Now, the *Damascus Document*, which we unfortunately cannot date precisely, but which was

---

8    Of particular interest is the observation of M.O. Wise, *A Critical Study of the Temple Scroll*, pp. 35-59, that a Deuteronomic source may be detected in the Temple Scroll; the source he dates to the 3rd century BCE (pp. 58-59).

9    See my 'Sons of Cain', in J.D. Martin and P.R. Davies (eds), *A Word In Season. Essays in Honour of William McKane* (JSOTS, 42), Sheffield: JSOT Press, 1986, pp. 35-56.

composed quite probably within fifty years of Ben Sira either way, includes an historical review of Israel's early history (CD 2-3), which itemises acts of rebellion against God. The list opens with the 'heavenly watchers', followed by Noah, Abraham, Isaac and Jacob. A mixing of what were known to be 'biblical' and 'non-biblical' items is of course not to be ruled out.[10] But if so, it is significant that the authors did not care to distinguish between 'biblical' and 'non-biblical' sources in their arguments from history. More probable is either that they drew the border lines differently (including Enochic material in their 'scripture') or, as I think Ben Sira's allusions (above) tend to confirm, that Enoch material in Genesis was once more extensive than in the MT.

The case of the Joseph story is also worth a look. Ben Sira, as we have seen, omits Joseph from his survey until he introduces him at the end, in a final strophe, which reverses the chronological order and alludes to Enoch, Joseph, Shem, Seth and Adam. But Joseph is out of sequence, and is remembered only for his bones being 'cared for': there is no allusion to his success in Egypt, or his ability to decipher dreams, which one might expect from Ben Sira. The allusion is certainly suspicious, and it makes one wonder whether it is primary or secondary, and, even if it is primary, what Ben Sira knew about Joseph at all. The Joseph story, after all, has long been recognized as formally different from the preceding patriarchal stories; von Rad held it to be a wisdom tale;[11] it has been compared with the tales of Daniel and Esther,[12] and Noth took it to be a relatively late linkage between his Pentateuchal patriarchal and exodus themes.[13] How late might this link have been?

There are other places in the Masoretic biblical text which it is reasonable to think may have achieved their present form later than the 2nd century BCE. In the passage just alluded to from the *Damascus Document*, there is a reference to 'Egypt' but not to Joseph, and the

10   Note too that CD does appear to allude to the book of Jubilees at 16.3, though neither the citation nor the argument from it do not imply that Jubilees is seen as 'scriptural'

11   G. von Rad, 'The Joseph Narrative and Ancient Wisdom', *The Problem of the Hexateuch and Other Essays*, ET Edinburgh: Oliver and Boyd, 1966, pp. 292-300.

12   The most recent discussion of these narratives, and the genre, is that of L.M. Wills, *The Jew in the Court of the Foreign King* (HDR, 26), Minneapolis: Fortress Press, 1990.

13   M. Noth, *A History of Pentateuchal Traditions*, pp. 208-213.

Israelites in Egypt are said to have sinned, which, again, does not correspond with the Masoretic account. The positive picture of Adam in both Ben Sira and the Dead Sea Scrolls, indeed, implied in much of the pseudepigraphic literature, may suggest that the Eden story of Genesis 2–3 is a very late amendment to an account of the origin of sin that may have included the descent of the Watchers. Specifically, Ben Sira 17.7,11, referring to the creation of mankind, and in either ignorance or contradiction of Genesis 2-3 says:[14]

> He filled them with knowledge and understanding
> and showed them good and evil...
> He bestowed knowledge upon them
> and allotted to them the law of life.

The nearest that Ben Sira comes to hinting at Gen. 2-3 is at 25.24 (Heb. 23) where the Hebrew[15] reads *m'šh thlt 'wn wgllh gw'nw yḥd*, which several, perhaps the majority of commentators take to be a reference to Eve.[16] This is pretty unconvincing: the context of the statement (25.13-26.18) makes it clear that women generally are a source of sin (which is a common theme of wisdom writing), and the man who gets a good wife is indeed blessed (26.1: 'twice lengthened are his days').

What I have said up to this point has aimed at establishing two things in particular. One is that we are better avoiding the term 'scripture' when dealing with a strictly historical problem; we can instead observe how writers in the first centuries BCE and CE refer to two bodies of literature generally called by them 'law' and prophets'. The tendency to use either 'law' (4 Ezra) or 'prophets' (Josephus) as a universal category is a late first-century CE phenomenon which points to the development of a notion of a self-contained and cohesive body of religiously authoritative writing. However, in 4 Ezra the exclusive religious authority of the twenty-four books is in doubt, since seventy other books have more value, while Josephus, on the other hand, does seem to need to justify the status of the twenty-two, though he has to do it by the rather specious device of denying the existence, since the

14  Cf. 33.10-13; 40.1; 41.8-9 speaks of being 'born to a curse' but only of 'ungodly men'.

15  I am using the Geniza text here (*The Hebrew Text of the Book of Ecclesiasticus*, ed. I. Lévi, Leiden: Brill, 1951). The Masada text does not include this passage.

16  E.g. P. Skehan and A. DiLella, *The Wisdom of Ben Sira* (AB), Garden City: Doubleday, 1987, pp. 348-49 (see also the references given there).

time of Artaxerxes, of a reliable historical record due to failure of prophetic succession–which does not prevent him from using such books for his own history. But before that time, the boundaries between the 'law and/or prophets' on the one hand, and other literature on the other hand, are not consistently maintained, and it is not clear, for example, that the five scrolls of Moses are always understood to be 'the law', since there is also one scroll of the 'law of Moses'. The picture is patchy, and points to a convergence towards consensus but not a consensus as yet. Josephus sees the prophetic books as history, Philo sees them differently; somewhat earlier, Hecataeus of Abdera (end of the 4th century), had known simply of Jewish books relating 'the establishment and the constitution' of the Jews'.[17] Other non-Jewish and Jewish writers regarded Judaism as a philosophy and their books as works of philosophy.[18] In other words, we can agree that there is more or less a corpus of literature which defines Judahism, but there is a range of attitudes regarding its exact significance (perhaps corresponding to a range of opinions about what being a Judahite/Jew really meant). My second point is that we should not assume *either* the contents of the 'prophets' *or* of the 'law' to be fixed by the beginning of the second century BCE, nor that either collection had an agreed or defined religious status.

### From cultural archive to religious tract

Can we therefore usefully deploy the term 'scripture' or the concept that it implies in dealing with the period between, say, 200 BCE and the end of the first century CE? I think that we can accept the implied distinction between 'scripture' and 'literature' by recognizing a difference between on the one hand regarding the literature as a cultural resource, a venerable body of ancient texts, comparable if not superior to the classics of Greece, and on the other hand espousing it as a religious resource, a collection of statements from God about the way in which a Judaistic/Jewish life should be led.[19] Perhaps even this distinction is too rigid, and attitudes between these two positions must

17   See E. Bickerman, *The Jews in the Greek Age*, Cambridge: Harvard University Press, 1988, pp. 16-17.

18   See, *inter alia*, J. Goldstein, *I Maccabees* (AB), New York: Doubleday, 1984, pp. 129-31.

19   The distinction will not work in every case, perhaps. Philo might be argued to have it both ways. But that is Philo's method.

be allowed–in which case, perhaps, the term 'scripture' cannot have a strict.connotation. But even that overdrawn distinction is effective only when one can speak of a way of life which is religious, whether of a society governed by a divine law, or an individual or group adopting its contents as a moral imperative for personal piety. 'Scripture' can only exist as a *notion* only where there has evolved *a religious system which permits 'scripture' to have a function*. We cannot ask in chicken-and-egg fashion whether 'Judaism' or 'scripture' came first. We can only ask in what way a religious system, or, better, a set of related religious systems, and a body of literature interacted and in so doing defined each other. What I am trying to trace in this chapter is a strengthening of the relationship between how Jews/Judaeans defined their identity and their national literature. In so doing, I shall confine myself to Palestine, since it is not clear to me how wide a range of religious behaviour, and what criteria, might have passed for 'Judaism' in the Diaspora.

The ways in which the biblical literature in the late Persian-Hellenistic period came to be used for religious purposes, whether national, communal or individual, are varied and hard to evaluate. In some cases focus is on the legal contents as a basis for obedience to the commands of Yahweh; in other cases the 'way of Yahweh' entails something broader. What unites all these attitudes is a commitment to fulfilling the will of the deity and a belief that this will is communicated, whether or not exclusively, in the writings. Furthermore, these developments attest the emergence of religious lifestyles of various kinds, going beyond mere participation in a cult or the observance of traditional norms of behaviour. One might even say that in the sense in which we often use the term today, we are seeing the emergence of religion, something embraced by iindividual choice and constituted by commitment. Such personal attitudes towards religion may not have been entirely unknown before the arrival of Hellenistic culture in the Levant, but they are certainly very typical of it.

However, the reasons for this development of attitudes towards national culture and religion are, I think, many and complex. On inspection several considerations need to be taken into account, and even cumulatively they hardlty exhaust the possibilities.

## 1. *Arrival of the Greeks*

To explain this development it may be helpful and not too misleading to correlate this process with the gradual awareness of the Hellenistic world in Yehud. The centre of cultural gravity in the region moves from east to west, and the Judaeans, like their neighbours (except perhaps the Phoenicians, who had always looked west as well as east), encounter a people of a strange language, with strange gods and a novel set of attitudes: these Greeks find circumcision curious, even comic, nudity natural, homosexuality normal, gods interchangeable. And they are everywhere, too–trading, fighting, settling down, building their cities, opening their schools, preaching their ideas. Unlike previous empires, this one is tending towards a homogeneous culture. Its values do not impose themselves externally so much as invite convergence with local cultures. I will not venture any more here into Hellenism: it is a complex and even disputed topic, and not suited to much generalization. But that it had profound, if gradual and complex, effects upon the culture of Yehud is quite evident. The attraction and pervasiveness of the new culture combined with internal processes to create amongst many citizens of the Levant a conscious reaction, a resistance, a strengthening of feeling for a distinct national culture. While the religious beliefs and practices of Yehud were at first quite consistent with Persian religious ideas, and perhaps even with neighbouring cultures who also had their high god (a correspondence often mooted, and as often denied),[20] the advent of Greek-speaking traders and mercenaries, then cities and schools and Greek-speaking overlords provoked a sense of cultural insecurity, which crystallized into two typical reactions: the one to adapt to the new style of being and practise a 'Judaism' that was consistent with it. The other was to react against the new culture and in so doing to appeal to a traditional 'Judaism'[21].It is this 'traditional Judaism' which I wish to focus on here. How, and to what extent, had a recognizable way of being Judaean/Jewish developed by this time? One can certainly appeal to the cult of the Jerusalem temple and the

20  For a convenient recent review on Persian influence on the Bible, though with an overly negative conclusion, Yamauchi, *Persia and the Bible*; on Syrian and Palestinian religion, see Niehr, *Der höchste Gott*.

21  I use this word cautiously, since there can hardly be said to be a single Judaism in this period, in the sense of a religion. But I use the term quite deliberately, since the religious sense, I think, derives from a cultural sense, in which 'Judaism' means the culture of Judah/Yehud, however that is defined.

religious ethos which surrounded it. It was what was perceived as an attack on this cult that seems to have finally triggered a revolt of some Judaeans against Antiochus IV. But we are not speaking merely of a cult, but of a culture. According to the books of Maccabees, distinctive of the Judaean way of life was circumcision, abstinence from pork and the veneration of certain books. And in speaking of a culture, we are probably referring to those to whom such things mattered: the ruling and merchant classes and not the peasants. Why would it matter to these people? One obvious answer is that for the Greeks the notion of a society ruled by priests was odd. The economic, social and political system of Judah was threatened by a different set of values, which could either be accommodated or resisted. Those anticipating greater power as a result would tend to embrace it, those fearing loss of power would resist; and this is indeed the dynamic which led to the so-called Maccabean revolt. It appears to have been conducted partly on the basis of an appeal to such a traditional culture; certainly the Jewish literature represents it in these terms, though they are translated into religious values. To put it crudely, the encroachment of Hellenistic ideas induced the kind of nationalistic fundamentalism with which our own century is familiar, even to the extent of adopting values that are only *thought* to have been traditional. From the writing of the biblical literature and its adoption of it as a national cultural index, or as a scripture, this broad cultural development played a role in shaping that development.

## 2. *Scribal education*

Scribes learning to write the *Bildungssprache* (what we call 'Hebrew' was chosen no doubt as part of the claim to be the descendants of the earlier Israelites and Judaeans) were taught from texts in that language, written by their fathers and grandfathers. Whether or not in antagonism to Greek culture, Moses replaced Homer, Solomon Amenemopet, Qoheleth Plato and Job Sophocles–though the choice may not have been exclusive. This does not, of course of itself establish the literature as having some *religious* authority, though naturally the national culture is defined strongly in religious categories, since the temple is the centre of economic and political life. In accordance with most ancient societies, ethics is equated with the divine will, history moves according to divine guidance, and the cult is conducted by divinely revealed rules, just as disease is divinely provoked and famine divinely prompted, neither of which makes either medicine or agriculture necessarily the basis of a religious lifestyle. Ben Sira treats the biblical writings as containing divine wisdom, but then he feels that his own efforts also aspire to that status. His religion is based on a simple morality and veneration for the cult. The will of his deity is certainly to be discovered in the litertaure, just as it is in the cult and in everyday life. Writers like him, such as the authors of Daniel, the author of 1 Maccabees, or of the Enochic books, or of the Genesis Apocryphon, (or even Jubilees), did not apparently see a difference between the process of reading the existing literature and adding to it or even modifying what it said. For a scribe to read, copy and amend was part of the same process, and to comment on, likewise, in the form of supplementary books. The literature, in the eyes of many of these authors and writers is a cultural resource, but not a foundation for a religious lifestyle. These writers are not 'theologians'. It is often quoted, it is highly venerated, but these attitudes merely establish the literature as a benchmark of cultural identity and good education. The distinction between writers such as these and their predecessors who actually produced the biblical literature itself is not a sharp one at all; did Ben Sira or the writer of 1 Maccabees understand any such distinction? Did they perhaps know perfectly well that the biblical books were continuing to be copied and even slightly emended in their own days (even by themselves?) After all, they did succeed in having their own writings added to the corpus, if only in the end in the Greek edition!

Nevertheless, it can be said that the contents of the biblical scrolls had largely ceased to develop (though remaining textually variable); the writing is virtually over.The scrolls have been composed, emended and expanded, but a limit has been more or less reached. This is partly because their evolution has been affected in its final stages by factors such as the physical size of the scroll, the saturation point of a narrative, and the ever wider dissemination of the literature .While the original scrolls of Samuel or Kings perhaps had to become two (this is only a guess: the names themselves are not necessarily an indication that the separate scrolls were even united), the individual scrolls stopped growing for purely natural reasons. There comes a point beyond which further major attempts to perfect the product cease. The writing of books continues, of course: Eccl. 12.9-12 notes that of the making of books there is no end, and further scribal activity in the schools will take mostly the form of new compositions. Why the number of scrolls stops expanding is something I shall consider in the next chapter. But once the task of producing a national archive has been completed, a history has been written, suitable collections of wisdom and oracular poetry and religious hymns have been established, several things result. One is a lack of interest in meddling further; another is the onset of experimentation with new forms of literary output (such as we seen in the Dead Sea Scrolls and the Pseudepigrapha); another, however, is the tendency to view the inherited corpus in a more reverent way. Once a national history and literary archive have been produced, the next thing to do is to treat them as antique. A work of art in a painter's studio or a manuscript score on a composer's piano will in our own culture become sacrosanct as a work of art in a gallery or a score, over which critics and conductors will pore as holy products. The literature simply becomes more and more venerated and with each new generation the presumed date of origin of the scrolls recedes another few centuries. What is old contains truth, and the older the truer. In this way the move towards religious veneration is facilitated.

### 3. *Written law as an authority independent of the establishment*
One obvious way in which the literature moves towards 'scriptural' status, i.e. acquiring religious authority, is by being adopted as legally regulative. I do not want to enter into the vexed question of whether we have lawcodes in the Bible. The stories in Ezra and Nehemiah which describe the imposition (willingly accepted) of a law upon the people is almost certainly a later retrojection. But as such, it is an important indicator of a key development. What is increasingly recognized by scholars of biblical law as having been originally an exercise in legal theory, a wisdom text, a philosophical exercise, comes to be regarded as law to be applied, and applied religiously. The story of Ezra's reading of the law of Moses presupposes that either Deuteronomy or the books of Moses were to be understood as actual laws by which Judaeans were expected to live. And so the authors of Ezra believed, though how widespread was their view we cannot know. Certainly, Judah had been governed by laws, and the cult performed according to rules. But had the literature been appealed to as an arbiter in either situation? I suspect not, and not least because those who wrote the literature and those who made and knew

the rules were the same group. With the dissemination of the literature, other groups come into play, and within this widening circle are those who can use the written laws against the practices that they see in operation. And where they see the difference, they will accuse the authorities of departing from the will of the deity. Precisely this is what we find among the Dead Sea Scrolls.

Perhaps it is worth reiterating that the biblical laws are impossible to apply without the massive body of interpretation we find in the Mishnah and Talmud. The biblical 'law' comprises individual pieces or sets of legislation (concerning runaway slaves, for instance), theoretical principles (how to deal with Canaanite cities), cultic descriptions (the building of the Tabernacle); and includes accounts of how festivals and sacrifices should be offered. But the material as a whole is characterized by incompleteness (no law on divorce, only on remarrying one's former wife after she has been married to another); by contradiction or inconsistent duplication. There are different calendars, different times for the New Year, and different sets of technical terminology. Had these laws functioned, or had any authority wished to systematize them, this would have taken place. As it is, there are signs of harmonization here and there, but no indication of a need for practical enforcement. The adoption of the biblical 'laws' as 'real' laws to be operated, and obeyed, even the understanding of Judaism as a system of legal obedience, is a distinct step taken later than the composition of the literature, and even when taken, as it was by various groups at the end of the Second Temple period, did not command general assent until the development of rabbinic Judaism, which undertook a systematic and philosophcially informed transformation of the biblical law into a definition of its own Judaism in the Babylonian Talmud.[22]

This general adoption of the biblical law as regulating Judaism, or, better, as being obligatory for all who professed to be 'Israel' was anticipated by some centuries by certain groups. The Qumran texts afford us an excellent example of this: the *Temple Scroll* harmonizes and extends biblical legislation; the *Damascus Document* describes a community which claims to be founded on true revelation of the law,

22  Here I am following the arguments of Jacob Neusner, whose voluminous output defies annotation. But his thesis that the Babylonian Talmud finally reconciles Mishnah and scripture seems to me persuasive. His demonstration that Mishnah is built independently of scripture is also extremely important for the description I am offering here of the place of 'scripture' in Second Temple Judaism.

lives its communal life by biblical laws and accuses the rest of 'Israel' of being deceived by Belial into disobedience. This latter charge is substantiated by quotation from the biblical literature, as if to imply that both inside and outside the community such appeal was valid. The so-called 'halakic letter', 4QMMT,[23] appears to be a list of disputed interpretations of biblical laws relating to purity. There were those who, in the Hellenistic period at any rate, took it upon themselves to apply these laws, with the aid of exegesis, and argue about their meaning with opponents. Perhaps it was the case that several priestly and scribal Judaeans were, during the Hellenistic period, becoming committed to looking practically at the legal portions of their literature and trying to live by them, to varying degrees. This being said, however, it must be recognized that we do not have evidence of one monolithic 'Judaism' defined by a 'Jewish law'. Such an attitude defines only one kind of 'Judaism'. Exactly why such groups emerged is not clear; I suspect a number of reasons must have contributed. But, as we now know, these groups cannot be said to be deviating from, or preserving, a 'normative' Judaism. They are instead in the process of defining for themselves a form of Judaism (Judaean culture and religion) which they believe to be the one true form as dictated by the deity. In pursuit of this they begin to invent the idea of a 'Jewish law' and equate it with what is written in the national literature. As I suggested earlier, the external pressure of an alien culture may have had something to do with such a flight to what was a kind of fundamentalism.

## 4. *A search for personal piety*

In addition to *groups* defining a legal lifestyle, individuals also began to read the literature for devotional purposes, though without necessarily adopting a literal obedience to its individual injunctions .There is some evidence even in the biblical literature itself that it was becoming understood as *torah*, lore, teaching of a religious nature. Thus, Psalm 1 suggests not only that piety is more than a matter of adopting the conventional and international clichés of wisdom, but involves studying the *torah* of Yahweh. Prosperity in life is not a matter of listening (Proverbs) or looking (Ecclesiastes) but

23 Unpublished to date: see E. Qimron and J. Strugnell, 'An Unpublished Halakhic Letter from Qumran', in J. Amitai (ed.), *Biblical Archaeology Today*, Jerusalem: IES, 1985, pp. 400-407, also in *Israel Museum Journal* 4 (1985), pp. 9-12; and cf. J.T. Milik, in DJD 3, pp. 221-25.

'meditating'. Whether in this, Psalm or any particular case, the
meaning of *torah* can be confined exclusively to a defined body of
literature, there can hardly be doubt that study of scrolls is a central
part of the new wisdom. Presumably, Psalm 1 presents the Psalms
collection itself as something for individual meditation. What is
equally clear from this instance, and even more so from Ps. 119 is
that this is a feature of *individual piety*. We are not encountering here
cultic conformity, not even legal conformity, but something more:
moral and ethical conformity–and to what? What is the 'fear of
Yahweh' that is the basis of wisdom? It surely defines an individual
lifestyle, since it is *wisdom* we are talking about and not 'holiness'
which, in the language of much of the biblical literature defines the
status of the nation as a whole.

The popularity of the Psalms as sources of quotation in the New
Testament and Qumran shows that they were studied for religious
purposes. But so were the prophetic books. What is to be made of the
epilogue to Hosea, which commends its contents as words for the wise
to understand and thus to walk in the 'ways of Yahweh'? And why is
Daniel reading Jeremiah? Why is the Ethiopian eunuch whom Philip
converts reading Isaiah? At the stage in which the biblical literature
generates piety it has acquired a new audience, a new function–and a
new set of meanings. It has been translated into Greek, in which
language the majority of its readers will encounter it. It is being more
widely read. From the standpoint of a particular kind of sociological
analysis, one might even say that the literature defines an area of
power separate from the temple and the priesthood and that, as with
the Reformation, it can be appealed to and used by groups opposed to
the establishment in order to exercise an independent power. Perhaps
the increasing appeal to the literature as the source of religious
authority by certain groups can be analyzed as a symptom of the
dissipation of power. But that kind of analysis would require another
study. At all events, access to a wider audience is another factor in the
adoption of the biblical literature as a religious norm. But the
development of personal piety may in the end be one of those factors
ultimately inaccessible to the historian. Religious instincts are never to
be excluded from human affairs, and the age was indeed one of
religious and philosophical questing, in which the discovery of the
biblical literature as a religious resource was one of the more
successful, rewarding and, indeed, enduring.

## Manticism

One important hermeneutical approach to the biblical literature attested in the second century BCE and onwards is what might be called the mantic. The ancient literature is construed as a set of divine signs, rather in the manner that in Babylonia entrails or oil on water or anomalous births or dreams or star constellations were taken as clues to divine secrets.Here the religious and the esoteric unite. Works such as the Melchizedek fragments from Qumran Cave 11 use texts from different scrolls (Leviticus, Deuteronomy, Psalms, Daniel) to interpret one another. The implication that the meaning of a text from one of these books may be understood from a text out of another suggests a belief that the books comprise a special, even perhaps exclusive, religious authority as a collection and not just individually. In the next chapter we need to ask how it came about that a particular *set* of scrolls was so defined. On the other hand a composition such as the Qumran Habakkuk *pesher* finds in the biblical text a concealed prediction of the future. Belief in inspired exegesis creates a new authority figure, the charismatic teacher of mysteries, the interpreter, the Joseph, the Daniel, the 'teacher of righteousness'. If manticism itself is an ancient superstition, the adoption of the biblical literature as ancient wisdom, full of secrets of the past and future, gave it a new arena. And inspired words of the ancients became words of the deity, oracles, as Philo calls them. Thus, instead of the ancient prophets uttering words from the deity, the whole prophetic book itself becomes the 'word of God'. That particular hermeneutical move demonstrates as clearly as anything the shift from literature as ancient and venerable human culture and literature as eternal divine truth. Between the two are cultural developments that it is the responsibility of the biblical scholar to explore rather than to obliterate by theologically-inspired obfuscation.

## Conclusions

Our fairly recently-acquired understanding of Judaean religion in this period as variegated, and comprising several parties, sects and philosophies, with no orthodoxy other than authorized sanctuary procedures, which could themselves change as the priestly families dictated, enables me to suggest that the role of the biblical literature between 200 BCE and 70 CE (to take convenient dates) was also variegated. To some groups the literature was what we would call scriptural: to others not. As an outstanding example of a group seeking to apply the literature as law and define a religious lifestyle for itself I am tempted to suggest the Pharisees, the authors of the *Damascus Document* and also the members of the *yahad*. The Enochic material suggests, though no more, the possibility of a kind of Judaism to which the biblical literature was loosely attached in any religious sense. At all events, if one cannot speak of the biblical writings as the 'faith of Israel', then neither can one speak of them as the 'scriptures of Judaism'–not, that is, until a good deal later. There remain forms of Judaism in which the biblical literature played a lesser part, though never less than a treasured one. It is also to be recognized that different parts of that literature functioned scripturally for different parties and individuals: laws for certain communities, and perhaps cultic laws for priestly parties, psalms especially for some individuals, and prophets for many different kinds. The flexibility of the biblical heritage is shown in the extent to which parties could disagree about the definition of 'Judaism' and its accommodation to Hellenism. It needs to be remembered that those much-maligned 'Hellenisers' anticipated in large measure what was to be accepted as Judaism by most self-styled Jews outside Palestine (and within). The liturgical use of the scripture is a vexed question into which I have not ventured. When did synagogues begin to function? When was a habit of reading the scriptures introduced? One can imagine that in the diaspora the biblical literature would assume a greater importance as a symbol of Judaism, but how far was this really the case? If it is true that the literature created the identity 'Israel' to which a Jew could relate, and which in a fundamental way defined what being Judaean meant, we have to recognize that there is very little sign of this cultural archive succeeding in creating any significant uniformity in Jewish religious definition. It remained, as far as I can see, an adherence to a single god, avoidance of idols, circumcision, sabbath observance and going to the *proseuchē* that defined the diaspora Jew, and very little application of 'scriptural' norms. Only with rabbinic Judaism and Christianity do we confront 'biblical' religions; before that fundamental appeals to the religious authority of scripture are the mark of a sectarian, or, if the term be strictly inappropriate, an extremist.

Chapter Nine

## THE EMERGENCE OF ISRAEL

This book, which started by driving a thick wedge between the literary and the historical 'Israel', fittingly concludes with the convergence, however partial and brief, of historical and literary manifestations. Under the Hasmonaeans a Judaean state flowered momentarily, and it was a state which owed as much to the biblical literature as it did to political fortune. The Hasmonaeans must be seen as the nearest that Judah ever approached to the ideal enshrined in its literature: a monarchic state stretching over most of Palestine, and defeating its neighbours, the erstwhile Ammonites, Moabites and Edomites, as well as inflicting revenge, finally, on the erstwhile kingdom of Israel by destroying the Samaritan sanctuary. Not least important, the focus of this state was on the sanctuary in its capital, Jerusalem. These coincidences are neither ironic nor unintentional. The Hasmonaean state was a deliberate attempt at reviving the past (albeit to the historian an unreal past). The writer of 1 Maccabees at least is quite aware of this dimension, being at pains to utilize the biblical resonances to tell the story of a family of charismatic deliverers, judges 'raised up' by the deity to deliver the people from the nations 'round about' who were seeking to exterminate them.

But the connection between the Hasmonaeans and the biblical literature runs also in the other direction. The Hasmonaeans almost certainly had an important role to play in the process by which this literary heritage achieved a national, official and finally authoritative status.[1] It is well-known that while the successors of the Maccabees fairly rapidly assumed the character of a Hellenized dynasty, they had risen to their prominence with the aid of religious groups. They themselves, and their supporters, fought a war of resistance on grounds that were not entirely or purely religious, but which focussed

1    On the role of the Maccabees in furthering Judaism, see now P. Haas, 'The Maccabean Struggle to Define Judaism', in J. Neusner *et al.* (eds), *New Perspectives on Ancient Judaism* (BJS, 206), Atlanta: Scholars Press, 1990, pp. 49-65.

on the Temple and on other religious symbols. The books of Maccabees certainly strive to present the war as a religious one, and refer in particular to a group they call *Ḥasidim* or 'Hasidaeans' *(asidaioi)*. In 1 Maccabees, these join with Judas and later secede, while in 2 Maccabees they comprise Judas's followers throughout. Whatever the identity of these people, or their aims, both writers describe a major group in the armed resistance bearing a religious label, 'pious'. It is a name used in the biblical literature, particularly in the Psalms, to denote those whom I described in the previous chapter who read the biblical literature in aid of personal piety.[2] Whether the Hasmonaeans themselves were religious in their motivation is for historians to speculate. The story of Mattathias and his raising of the revolt is hardly to be accepted as anything more than a legend spread by his family and supporters (including the author of 1 Maccabees) and inspired by Numbers 25 (to which Mattathias's following speech alludes). As a priestly family (or thus they claimed) the sons of Mattathias may have had a marginal interest in the priestly struggle for the highest office, one which they were subsequently able to fill. In the context of a newly-won political autonomy, the authority which they also monopolised made them vulnerable to religious pressure groups (such as the Pharisees, according to Josephus) and having fought on a religious principle, they will have been faced with demands to promote certain religious interests.

Ironically, it was probably Antiochus IV's attack on the cult and religious symbols of Judah that did much to further the identification of religion and culture. The Hasmonaeans were thereafter in a position, then, and somewhat under an unavoidable obligation, to give increased political status to religious issues, and to advance to a national status what was previously the agenda of a religious party or parties. Sabbath observance, circumcision, diet, tithing, regulation festivals–all these, whatever their prehistory in various religious organizations, can now become part of the official religion of Judaeans. Such a public definition will also explain the extent to which Judaean culture/Judaism preserved a minimal common denominator (and what that was remains disputed!) throughout the Roman, and Parthian, empires. For it is probably during the Hasmonaean period that an impetus was given to the dissemination of 'Judaism' well beyond the borders even of the forcibly enlarged boundaries of a

2    On the problem of the *Ḥasidim*, see my 'Ḥasidim in the Maccabean Period', *JSS* 28 (1977), pp. 127-140.

'greater Judaea'. The Diaspora did not acquire its Jewish culture from the sixth century BCE in Babylon and Egypt. It can only have absorbed it over the centuries during which it came into being, especially during the great population exports from Judah which had perhaps accelerated during the Ptolemaic and Seleucid periods and culminated in the missionary zeal of Herod the Great, who, whatever his Palestinian subjects thought of him, probably created more Jewish converts outside Palestine than any other single figure by his tireless patronage, showing that Judaism was a respectable and philhellenic philosophy, worthy of adoption by the most sophisticated and intellectual Greek. The extent to which Judaism spread by adoption is still probably underestimated. And who knows, but for Constantine, whether it might have finally conquered Rome instead of its sibling?

The heightening of political and religious consciousness during the Maccabaean and Hasmonaean period at the same time revealed the lack of consensus on either politics or religion. What is dramatized in the books of Maccabees (and in many modern history books) as a split between 'traditionalists' and 'progressives' remained on the national agenda, and the struggle to secure 'orthodoxy' for one part of the spectrum over another began–a struggle resolved in a certain manner only with the formal triumph of rabbinic Judaism, for which loss of the temple as a focus of power was probably a strict prerequisite. In short, the Hasmonaeans won their war with the aid of those who were religiously motivated, let them down rather quickly afterwards, but could not avoid the need to adjudicate in the ensuing religious debate.

## *The Hasmonaean library*

The Hasmonaeans were obviously eager to use religious symbols and slogans themselves in furtherance of their dynastic ends. Their propagandist, the writer of 1 Maccabees, expresses such claims, their own coinage certainly suggests as much, and the destruction of the Samaritan temple, however much politically expedient, was surely exploited as a religious gesture. However, the subject of interest is their attitude towards the national literature, what many of their supporters were treating as 'scripture'. According to 2 Macc. 2.13, 'just as Nehemiah collected the chronicles of the kings, the writings of prophets, the works of David and royal letters about sacred offerings, to found his library, so Judas also has collected all the books that had been scattered...', apparently after Antiochus (according to 1 Macc. 1.56-7) had tried to destroy them The final item aside, (and Ezra 1.1-4 [note v. 4 especially] looks like such a letter: perhaps the reference is to an as yet incomplete book of Ezra?), his statement can be interpreted to mean that in the author's day there existed in Jerusalem a library of books which were thought to have been there since the time of Nehemiah, and which correspond very well with what is in the biblical literature. The act of setting up such an archive (whether by Judas or one of his successors) deserves evaluation in the context of Hasmonaean policy, and, of course, as an important step in the establishment of the literature as a 'scripture' for 'Judaism'.

Whether or not Beckwith is correct in deducing that the term 'holy writings' implies their storage in a holy place, namely the temple,[3] and to what extent an archive had existed previously, we can surmise that the act of creating this library amounted to a decision about the authority of certain books. Restoring or creating a royal or temple library was not in itself remarkable. Such an institution had a long history in the ancient Near East and was being extended in the Hellenistic world even to private libraries. There had been libraries at Mari, Ugarit (where there were two, a government archive and a temple one) and Tell el-Amarna; also at Edfu, where all that was left was a catalogue on the library walls. Memphis had a medical library; Ashur, Ur, Nippur and Kish had libraries. The Assyrians may have been the first archivists: Ashurbanipal's librarians grouped the documents by subject and catalogued them by lettering them on the outside, often consecutively numbering them in the case of longer compositions. In the fourth century BCE there was a library at Athens, while Alexandria had one in the third century BCE too, apparently including Greek translations of foreign works, including some from Judah. Antiochus III (also third century) established one at Antioch (whose librarian was called Euphorion of Chalcis); Pergamon had one in the mid-second century BCE. Libraries were matters of public and personal pride, often taken as spoils by Romans (who introduced public libraries).

It is correct, then, to see the establishment of a library by the Hasmonaeans in the context of an established practice, but perhaps even more importantly in the closer context of an assertion of national identity in an increasingly cosmopolitan world. Since copies of the

3    Beckwith, 'Formation of the Hebrew Bible', pp. 40-45.

biblical scrolls had been in circulation previously, and there existed Greek translations of most of these, the point of such a library is hardly preservation (as 2 Maccabees ingenuously implies). But reasons of state do not exhaust the explanation for this library. In alluding to the biblical literature, Josephus (*Ant.* 3.38; 5.61) refers to it as 'held in the temple', and also, as we saw in the previous chapter, insists that the Jews have only twenty-two books. Since he knows of, and uses, other Jewish books, he is obviously referring to a particular and defined collection–unless he is making up the figure (and it is not the same figure as 4 Ezra gives!). Such a collection cannot be imposed except by an appropriate authority nor easily maintained except through an established archive. The Hasmonaean temple library of Jewish/Judaean books is the obvious moment for such a definitive corpus to be established and indeed to remain as the definitive corpus. What is 'in' the Jewish 'scriptures' can henceforth mean what is housed as such in the temple library. Perhaps this state of affairs was only.consequential, but I doubt that the Hasmonaeans, in view of the circumstances of their rise to power outlined earlier, did not give careful thought to what should thereby be officially sanctioned and what excluded.

Establishment of a norm also defines what is abnormal, and orthodoxy what is unorthodox. In other libraries, the preservation, and even copying of the texts of the law and the prophets continued for some time without regard to the content or the text of the temple scrolls, and indeed, perhaps in outright defiance of the temple authorities. It is not impossible that the deposition of scrolls at Qumran has something to do with the creation of scribal schools and libraries which perpetuated traditions and practices now excluded from the Jerusalem cult, temple and library, regardless of whether they also represent in some measure the literature of distinct communities. The establishment of such an archive, then, entails the possibility of fixing a definitive version, both as to content and to text, of the literature of Judah, or of 'Israel'. From this moment we might expect to find traces in Hebrew manuscripts of revision in accordance with an official version, while we would also expect to find evidence of a lack of uniformity in text from before this time. The evidence from Qumran certainly supports such a proposal, though one should be wary of claiming this too eagerly since we would have no reason to assume that a segregated community would pay attention to a standard text over their own. Yet, we do not know that the biblical texts stem from any one community, nor the date of the establishment of any community. It is quite possible that the Qumran hoard (or is it hoards?) represent the contents of a number of libraries, and again it is tempting to consider whether the texts preserved here include those which were officially disfavoured by the Hasmonaeans and excluded from their Temple library.

Thus, quite apart from the late rabbinic tradition about the three copies of the law kept in the Temple,[4] we have the observation of Josephus, quoted in the last chapter, that 'we do not possess myriads of inconsistent books conflicting with each other...'. The determination of the contents of the official list, as well as the text of the constituent scrolls in such a library explains why from the end of the second century BCE the biblical literature stops growing and why we can trace the from this time the gradual process of fixing a standard text, with new Greek translations of the Hebrew being undertaken.

But perhaps the most dramatic evidence in connection with this enterprise is that the chronology now evident in the Masoretic text points to the rededication of the Temple under the Maccabees as a pivotal date.[5] Such a revision of the chronology suggests a deeper motivation on the part of the ruling dynasty. Not only does the new archive promote an official national history, a national archive and potentially a normative literature for religious purposes, but, as revised by the Hasmonaean scribes, the literature is presented as being now fulfilled. The constitution of the biblical laws is being realized through the patronage of the king-priests, and the history of 'Israel' being brought to a glorious climax in the establishment of Judaean/Israelite hegemony in the Promised Land. As an historical and literary creation, the Bible, though not yet properly to be spoken of as such, is a Hasmonaean concept. The Hebrew Bible, the Masoretic consonantal text, are both the products of this politically ambitious dynasty.

It is likely that to the Hasmonaeans we should also attribute other processes of 'normativization'. A single official Judaean calendar, including the liturgical cycle is probably their doing, together with a

4    L Finkelstein, *Sifre on Deuteronomy*, New York: Ktav, 1969, p. 423 (356).

5    See T.L. Thompson, *The Historicity of the Patriarchal Narratives* (BZAW, 133), Berlin: de Gruyter, 1974, p. 15; J. Hughes, *Secrets of the Times: Myth and History in Biblical Chronology* (JSOTS, 66), Sheffield: JSOT Press, 1990, pp. 234-35.

single official Temple cultic practice. Perhaps even the institution of the synagogue, in which the character of 'Judaism'; could be internalized by the population, was created by them. They are certainly entitled to claim a major role in the formation of 'Judaism' as the culture of what was for the first and the only time that Judah formed a complete and independent political state.

And thus, the final shaping of the Bible, as it could later be called, was an integral part of the constitution, historically, of 'Israel' in Hellenistic Judah. It was in the name of that 'Israel' that the Jews fought Rome, and of that 'Israel' that the rabbis successfully achieved a non-political reconstitution. The fact that the library of this politically ambitious regime has since become a canon of scripture for one religion, part of a canon for another and religiously authoritative for a third is both an irony and a triumph. The pen is, indeed, mightier than the sword, fiction mightier than truth, and belief more important to human motivation than knowledge. Historians must surely know this. Once the practitioners of traditional biblical scholarship can also accept this comforting fact, relinquish their anguished hold on a real 'ancient Israel' and cease to practise a theologically-dictated form of historical criticism, the disciplines of both theology and history may be the better for it.

## BIBLIOGRAPHY OF WORKS CITED

G. Ahlström, *The History of Ancient Palestine*, Sheffield: JSOT Press, 1992.

—'The Origin of Israel in Palestine', *SJOT* 2 (1991), pp. 19-34.

R. Albertz, C. Thoma & H. Hübner, 'Israel I-III', in *Theologische Realenzyklopädie* 16, Berlin, 1986, 368-89

W.F. Albright, *The Biblical Period from Abraham to Ezra*, New York: Harper and Row, 1965, pp. 84-7.

Y. Amir, 'Authority and Interpretation of Scripture in the Writings of Philo', in Mulder (ed.),*Mikra*, pp. 421-53.

H.W. Attridge & J.J. Collins (eds) *Of Scribes and Scrolls*, Lanham: University Press of America, 1990.

J. Baines, 'Literacy and Ancient Egyptian Society', in *Man*, London: Royal Anthropological Institute of Great Britain and Ireland, 1983, pp. 572-99.

J. Barr, *Judaism–Its Continuity with the Bible* (The 7th Montefiore Memorial Lecture), University of Southampton, 1968.

—*Holy Scripture: Canon, Authority, Criticism*, London: SCM, 1983.

H. Barstad, *A Way in the Wilderness: the 'Second Exodus' in the Message of Second Isaiah*, Manchester: Manchester University Press, 1989.

J. Barton, *Oracles of God. Perceptions of Ancient Prophecy After the Exile*, London: Darton, Longman and Todd, 1986.

R.T. Beckwith, 'Formation of the Hebrew Bible', in Mulder (ed.), *Mikra*, pp. 39-86 (41).

E. Ben Zvi, 'History and Prophetic Texts', paper delivered at the 1991 Annual SBL Meeting, Kansas City (unpublished).

E.J. Bickerman, 'The Babylonian Captivity', in W.D. Davies and L. Finkelstein (eds), *The Cambridge History of Judaism I*, pp. 142-58.

—*The Jews in the Greek Age*, Cambridge: Harvard University Press, 1988.

J. Blenkinsopp, *Prophecy and Canon. A Contribution to the Study of Jewish Origins*, Notre Dame, University of Notre Dame Press, 1977.

—*A History of Prophecy in Israel: From the Settlement in the Land to the Hellenistic Period*, Philadelphia: Westminster, 1983, p. 227.

—'Temple and Society in Achaemenid Judah', in *Second Temple Studies*, pp. 22-53.

M. Boyce, *A History of Zoroastrainism*, Leiden: Brill, 1975.

—'Persian Religion in the Achemenid Age', in *CHJ* 1, pp. 279-307.

J.H. Breasted, *Ancient Records of Egypt IV*, Chicago: Chicago University Press, 1906-7; reprinted New York: Russell and Russell, 1962.

P. Briant, 'Villages et communautés villageoises d'Asie achéménide et hellénistique', *Journal for Economic and Social History of the Orient*, 18 (1975), pp. 165-88.

—'Appareils d'état et développement des forces productives au moyen-orient ancien: le cas de l'empire achéménide', *La Pensée*, February 1981, pp. 475-89.

M.G. Brett, *Biblical Criticism in Crisis*, Cambridge: CUP, 1991.

R.P. Carroll, 'Textual Strategies and Ideology in the Second Temple Period', in Davies (ed.), *Second Temple Studies*, pp. 108-124.

B.S. Childs, *Introduction to the Old Testament as Scripture*, London: SCM Press, 1979.

D.J.A. Clines, *What Does Eve Do To Help? and Other Readerly Questions to the Old Testament* (JSOTS, 94), Sheffield: JSOT Press, 1990.

—*et al.* (eds), *The Bible in Three Dimensions* (JSOTS, 87), Sheffield: JSOT Press, 1990, pp. 321-35.

R.B. Coote, *Early Israel. A New Horizon*, Minneapolis: Fortress, 1990.

R.B. Coote and K.W. Whitelam, *The Emergence of Israel in Historical Perspective* (SWBA, 5), Sheffield: Almond Press, 1987.

A.E. Cowley, *Aramaic Papyri of the Fifth Century B.C.*, Oxford: Clarendon Press, 1923.

F.M. Cross, 'Aspects of Samaritan and Jewish History in Late Persian and Hellenistic Times', *HTR* 59 (1966), pp.201-11.

M.A. Dandamaev, 'Achaemenid Babylonia', in I.M. Diakonoff (ed.), *Ancient Mesopotamia*, pp. 296-311.

G.A. Danell, *Studies in the Name Israel in the Old Testament*, Uppsala, 1945.

A. Danto, *Analytical Philosophy of History*, Cambridge: CUP, 1965.

G.I. Davies, *Ancient Hebrew Inscriptions*, Cambridge: CUP, 1992.

—*Megiddo* (Cities of the Biblical World), Guildford: Lutterworth Press, 1987.

P.R. Davies, (ed.) *Second Temple Studies* (JSOTS, 117), Sheffield: JSOT Presss, 1991.

—'Does Biblical Studies Need a Dictionary?' in D.J. Clines *et al.* (eds),*The Bible in Three Dimensions*, Sheffield: JSOT Press, 1990, pp. 321-35.

—'Sons of Cain' in J.D. Martin and P.R. Davies (eds) *A Word In Season*, pp. 35-56.

W.D. Davies and L. Finkelstein (eds), *The Cambridge History of Judaism I: Introduction; The Persian Period*, Cambridge: CUP, 1984.

W.D. Davies and L. Finkelstein (eds), *The Cambridge History of Judaism II: The Hellenistic Age*, Cambridge: CUP, 1989.

A. Demsky, 'Writing in Ancient Israel', in Mulder (ed.), *Mikra* , pp. 2-20.

I.M. Diakonoff (ed.), *Ancient Mesopotamia. Socio-Economic History: A Collection of Studies by Soviet Scholars*, Moscow: Nuaka, 1969.

D. Edelman, 'Introduction', *SJOT* 2 (1991), pp. 3-6.

T.C. Eskenazi, *In an Age of Prose. A Literary Approach to Ezra–Nehemiah* (SBLMS, 36), Atlanta: Scholars Press, 1988.

I. Finkelstein, *The Archaeology of the Israelite Settlement*, Jerusalem: IES, 1988.

—'The Emergence of Israel in Canaan: Consensus, Mainstream and Dispute', *SJOT* 2 (1991), pp. 47-59, 56.

L Finkelstein, *Sifre on Deuteronomy*, New York: Ktav\*\*, 1969.

M. Fishbane, *Biblical Interpretation in Ancient Israel*, Oxford: Clarendon Press, 1985.

—'Use, Authority and Interpretation of Mikra at Qumran', *Mikra*, pp. 339-377.

J.Fitzmyer, 'The Use of Explicit Old Testament Quotations in Qumran Literature and in the New Testament', *NTS* 7 (1960-1), pp. 297-333.

F.S. Frick, *The Formation of the State in Ancient Israel : A Survey of Models and Theories* (SWBA, 4), Sheffield: Almond Press, 1986.

J. Fowler, *Theophoric Personal Names in Ancient Hebrew* (JSOTS, 49), Sheffield: JSOT Press, 1988.

J.G. Gammie and L. Perdue (eds), *The Sage in Israel and the Ancient Near East*, Winona Lake: Eisenbrauns, 1990.

G. Garbini, *History and Ideology in Ancient Israel*, ET London: SCM Press, 1988.

D.W. Gooding, *Relics of Ancient Exegesis. A Study of the Miscellanies in 3 Reigns 2*, Cambrige, CUP, 1976.

J. Goldstein, *I Maccabees* (AB), New York: Doubleday, 1984.

N.K. Gottwald, *The Tribes of Yahweh. A Sociology of the Religion of Liberated Israel*, Maryknoll: Orbis, 1979.

D.M. Gunn, *The Story of King David: Genre and Interpretation* (JSOTS, 6), Sheffield: JSOT Press, 1978.

—*The Fate of King Saul: An Interpretation of a Biblical Story* (JSOTS, 14), Sheffield: JSOT Press, 1980.

J.M. Hadley, 'The Khirbet el-Qom Inscription', *VT* 37 (1987), pp. 50-62.

P.D. Hanson, *The People Called. The Growth of Community in the Bible*, San Francisco: Harper and Row, 1986.

M. Haran, 'Book-Scrolls in Israel in Pre-Exilic Times', *JJS* 33 (1982), pp. 161-73.

—'More Concerning Book-Scrolls in Pre-Exilic Times', *JJS* 35 (1984), pp. 84-5.

—'Book-Scrolls at the Beginning of the Second Temple Period: The Transition From Papyrus to Skins', *HUCA* 54 (1983), pp. 111-22.

J.H. Hayes, 'Israel,' *Mercer Dictionary of the Bible*, Macon, GA: Mercer Press, 1989, 417-20.

S. Herrmann, 'Operationen Pharao Schoschenks I. am östlichen Ephraim', *ZDPV* 80 (1964), pp. 55-79.

E. Hobsbawm and T. Ranger (eds), *The Invention of Tradition*, Cambridge: CUP, 1983.

K. Hoglund, 'The Achaemenid Context', in P.R. Davies (ed.), *Second Temple Studies*, pp. 54-72.

D. Hopkins, *The Highlands of Canaan: Agricultural Life in the Early Iron Age* (SWBA, 3), Sheffield: Almond Press, 1985.

J. Hughes, *Secrets of the Times: Myth and History in Biblical Chronology* (JSOTS, 66), Sheffield: JSOT Press, 1990.

A.R. Hulst, *Wat betekent de naam ISRAEL in het Oude Testament?*, 's-Gravenhaag, 1962.

A. Hurvitz, 'The Evidence of Language in Dating the Priestly Code', *RB* 81 (1974), pp. 24-56.

D.W. Jamieson-Drake, *Scribes and School in Monarchic Judah: A Socio-Archeological Approach* (SWBA, 9), Sheffield: Almond Press, 1991.

A. Jepsen and K.-D. Schunck, *Von Sinuhe bis Nabukadnezar*, 4th ed., Berlin: Evangelische Verlagstanstalt, 1988

Y. Kaufmann *The Religion of Israel* , ET Chicago: University of Chicago Press, 1960.

R.W. Klein, *Israel in Exile. A Theological Interpretation*, Philadelphia, 1979.

M. Kochavi (ed.), *Judaea, Samaria and the Golan: Archaeological Survey 1967-1968*, Jerusalem: The Survey of Israel, 1972 [Hebrew].

E. A. Knauf, 'War "Biblisch-Hebräisch" eine Sprache?', *ZAH* 3 (1990), pp. 11-23.

—review of G. Ahlström, *Who Were the Israelites?*, *JNES* 49 (1990), p. 82.

D. Kraemer, 'On the Relationship of the Books of Ezra and Nehemiah', *JSOT* [forthcoming]

H-J. Kraus, *Worship in Israel* , ET Oxford: Blackwell, 1965.

A. Kuhrt, 'The Cyrus Cylinder and Persian Imperial Policy', *JSOT* 25 (1983), pp. 83-97.

J. K. Kuntz, *The People of Ancient Israel. An Introduction to Old Testament Literature, History and Thought*, New York: Harper & Row, 1974.

N.-P. Lemche, *The Canaanites and their Land: The Tradition of the Canaanites* (JSOTS, 110), Sheffield: JSOT Presss, 1990.

I. Lévi, *The Hebrew Text of the Book of Ecclesiasticus*, Leiden: Brill, 1951.

W. McKane, *Jeremiah* (ICC), Edinburgh: T. and T. Clark, 1986.

O. Margalith, 'On the Origin and Antiquity of the Name Israel', *ZAW* 102 (1990), pp. 225-237.

J.D. Martin and P.R. Davies (eds), *A Word In Season. Essays in Honour of William McKane* (JSOTS, 42), Sheffield: JSOT Press, 1986.

A. Mazar, *Archaeology of the Land of the Bible* (AB), Garden City: Doubleday, 1990.

B. Mazar 'The Campaign of Pharaoh Shishak to Palestine', *SVT* 4 (1957), pp. 57-66.

A. Millard, 'An Assessment of the Evidence for Writing in Ancient Israel', *Biblical Archaeology Today*, Jerusalem: IES, pp. 301-12.

J.M. Miller and J.H. Hayes *A History of Ancient Israel and Judah*, Philadelphia: Westminster, 1986.

S. Mowinckel, *Studien zu dem Buche Esra-Nehemia*, Oslo: Universitetsforlaget, 1964.

J. Muilenburg, 'Form Criticism and Beyond', *JBL* 88 [1969], pp. 1-18.

M.J. Mulder (ed.), *Mikra* (CRINT II/1), Assen: Van Gorcum, 1988.

J. Neusner, B. Levine and E. Frerichs (eds) *Judaic Perspectives on Ancient Israel*, Philadelphia: Fortress, 1987.

E.W. Nicholson, *God and His People. Covenant and Theology in the Old Testament*, Oxford: Clarendon Press, 1986.

H. Niehr, *Der höchste Gott: Alttestamentlicher JHWH-Glaube im Kontext syrischkanaanäischer Religion des 1. Jahrtausends v. Chr.*(BZAW, 190), Berlin: De Gruyter, 1990.

M. Noth, *History of Israel*, ET London: A. & C. Black, 1951.

—*A History of Pentateuchal Traditions*, ET Englewood Cliffs: Prentice-Hall, 1972

M. O'Connor, 'The Poetic Inscription from Khirbet el-Qom', *VT* 37 (1987), pp. 224-30.

B. Oded, *Mass Deportations and Deportees in the Neo-Assyrian Empire*, Wiesbaden: Harrassowitz, 1979.

R. Oden, *The Bible Without Theology*, San Francisco: Harper and Row, 1987.

A.T. Olmstead, 'Darius as Lawgiver', *AJSL* 51 (1935), 247-49.

—*History of the Persian Empire*, Chicago: University of Chicago Press, 1948, pp. 119-342.

A.L. Oppenheim, *Letters from Mesopotamia*, Chicago: University of Chicago Press, 1967.

—'A Babylonian Diviner's Manual', *JNES* 33 (1974), pp. 174-220.

—'The Position of the Intellectual in Mesopotamian Society,' *Daedalus* 104/2, 1975, pp. 34-46.

E. Otto, *Rechtsgeschichte der Redaktion im Kodex E šnunna und in 'Bundesbuch'* (OBO, 85), Freiburg: Universitätsverlag, 1989.

G. Pettinato, *The Archives of Ebla*, Garden City: Doubleday, 1981, p.49.

B. Porten, in collaboration with J.C. Greenfield, *Jews of Elephantine and Aramaeans of Syene (Fifth Century BCE): Fifty Aramaic Texts with Hebrew and English Translations*, Jerusalem, 1974.

J. Pritchard (ed.), *Ancient Near Eastern Texts Relating to the Old Testament*, Princeton: Princeton University Press, 3rd ed., 1969.

E. Qimron, *The Hebrew of the Dead Sea Scrolls* (HSS, 29), Atlanta: Scholars Press, 1986.

E. Qimron and J. Strugnell, 'An Unpublished Halakhic Letter from Qumran', in J. Amitai (ed.), *Biblical Archaeology Today*, Jerusalem: IES, 1985.

G. von Rad, *Studies in Deuteronomy* (SBT, 9), London: SCM Press, 1953.

— 'The Joseph Narrative and Ancient Wisdom', *The Problem of the Hexatech and Other Essays*, ET Edinburgh: Oliver and Boyd, 1966.

D. B. Redford, 'The Ashkelon Relief at Karnak and the Israel Stele', *IEJ* 36 (1986), pp. 190-200.

— *Egypt, Canaan, and Israel in Ancient Times*, Princeton: Princeton University Press, 1992.

R. Rendtorff, *The Problem of the Process of Transmission of the Pentateuch* (JSOTS, 89), Sheffield: JSOT Press, 1990.

A. Rofé, 'The Battle of David and Goliath', in J. Neusner, *et al.* (eds), *Judaic Perspectives on Ancient Israel*, pp. 117-151.

J.W. Rogerson and P.R. Davies, *The Old Testament World*, Cambridge: CUP, 1989.

M.F. Rooker, *Biblical Hebrew in Transition: The Language of the Book of Ezekiel* (JSOTS, 90), Sheffield: JSOT Press, 1990.

S. Shaked, 'Iranian Influence on Judaism: First Century B.C.E. to Second Century B.C.E', *CHJ* 1, pp.308-25.

H. Shanks, 'When 5,613 Scholars Get Together in One Place: The Annual Meeting, 1990', *Biblical Archaeology Review* 17/2, March/April 1991, p. 66.

P. Skehan and A. DiLella, *The Wisdom of Ben Sira* (AB), Garden City: Doubleday, 1987.

D. Smith, *The Religion of the Landless*, Bloomington: Meyer-Stone, 1989.

Mark Smith, *The Early History of God*, San Francisco: Harper and Row, 1987.

Morton Smith, *Palestinian Parties and Politics That Shaped the Old Testament* 2nd edition, London: SCM Press, 1987.

—'II Isaiah and the Persians', *JAOS* 83 (1963), pp. 415-20.

L. Stager, 'Merenptah, Israel and Sea Peoples: new Light on an Old Relief', *Eretz Israel* 18 (1985), pp. 56-64.

E. Stern, *Material Culture of the Land of the Bible in the Persian Period*, Warminster: Aris and Phillips, 1982, p. 250.

H. Tadmor, 'The Origins of Israel as Seen in the Exilic and Post-Exilic Ages', in *Le Origini di Israele*, Rome: Accademia Nazionale dei Lincei, 1987, pp. 15-27.

T.L. Thompson, *The Historicity of the Patriarchal Narratives* (BZAW, 133), Berlin: de Gruyter, 1974.

—*The Origin Tradition of Ancient Israel: The Literary Formation of Genesis and Exodus 1– 23* (JSOTS, 55), Sheffield: JSOT Press, 1989.

—'From the Stone Age to Israel', *Proceedings of the Midwest Regional Meeting of SBL, 1991*, (forthcoming).

—*The Early History of the Israelite People : The Literary and Archaeological Evidence* (Studies in the History of the Ancient Near East, 2), Leiden: Brill, 1992.

C.C. Torrey, 'The Exile and the Restoration,' in *Ezra Studies*, Chicago: University of Chicago Press, 1910 (reprinted New York, Ktav, 1970), pp. 285-340.

J. Van Seters, *In Search of History. Historiography in the Ancient World and the Origins of Biblical History*, New Haven and London: Yale University Press, 1983.

J.D. Watts *Isaiah 34-66* (WBC) Waco:Word Books, 1987.

J. Weinberg, 'Demographische Notizen zur Geschichte der nachexilischen Gemeinde in Juda', *Klio* 59 (1972), pp. 45-59.

—'Das BEIT ABOTH im 6.-4. Jh. v. u. Z.', *VT* 23 (1973), pp. 400-14.

M. Weinfeld, *Deuteronomy and the Deuteronomistic School*, Oxford: Clarendon Press, 1972.

K.W. Whitelam, 'Between History and Literature: The Social Production of Israel's Traditions of Origin', *SJOT* 2 (1991), pp. 60-74.

R.N. Whybray, *The Intellectual Tradition in The Old Testament* (BZAW, 135), Berlin: De Gruyter, 1974.

—*The Making of the Pentateuch: A Methodological Study* (JSOTS, 53), Sheffield: JSOT Press, 1989

R.J. Williams, 'The Sage in Egyptian Literature', in J.G. Gammie and L. Perdue (eds), *The Sage in Israel and the Ancient Near East*, pp. 19-30 (27-29).

H.G.M. Williamson, 'The Concept of Israel in Transition,' in R.E. Clements (ed.) *The World of Ancient Israel*, Cambridge: CUP, 1989, pp. 141-159.

L.M. Wills, *The Jew in the Court of the Foreign King* (HDR,26), Minneapolis: Fortress Press, 1990.

D. Winton Thomas (ed.), *Documents from Old Testament Times*, Edinburgh: Nelson, 1958.

Michael O. Wise, *A Critical Study of the The Temple Scroll from Qumran Cave 11* (SAOC, 49), Chicago: Oriental Institute, 1990.

E. Yamauchi, *Persia and the Bible*, Grand Rapids: Baker Book House, 1990.

F.J. Yurco, 'Merenptah's Canaanite Campaign,' *Journal of the American Research Center in Egypt* 23 (1986), pp. 189-215.

# INDEX OF AUTHORS

## INDEX OF SOURCES

# JOURNAL FOR THE STUDY OF THE OLD TESTAMENT

## Supplement Series

## DATE DUE